Jeanne Darc

The patriot martyr and other narratives of female heroism in peace

Jeanne Darc

The patriot martyr and other narratives of female heroism in peace

ISBN/EAN: 9783742818867

Manufactured in Europe, USA, Canada, Australia, Japa

Cover: Foto ©Thomas Meinert / pixelio.de

Manufactured and distributed by brebook publishing software
(www.brebook.com)

Jeanne Darc

The patriot martyr and other narratives of female heroism in

peace

DEATH A VICTORY.

JEANNE DARC,

THE PATRIOT MARTYR:

AND

OTHER NARRATIVES

OF

FEMALE HEROISM IN PEACE AND WAR.

ILLUSTRATED.

LONDON:

BLACKIE & SON, 49 OLD BAILEY, E.C.;

GLASGOW, EDINBURGH, AND DUBLIN.

CONTENTS.

JEANNE DARC,

THE PATRIOT MARTYR.

INTRODUCTION.

THE pages of History are crowded with characters as the midnight sky is studded with stars. In both cases the variety is infinite. There are stars of all magnitudes, there are characters of all degrees; some shine with resplendent brilliancy, others are dim almost to obscurity. Among the greater historical luminaries few characters are more deserving of admiration than Joan of Arc. A simple peasant girl brooding over the misfortunes of her country until she persuaded herself, and ultimately persuaded others that she was divinely commissioned to repair them—heading an army inspired with enthusiasm by the nobility of her character and by her courage—marching from victory to victory till the avowed object of her mission was accomplished—desiring then to return to her original obscurity—betrayed at last into the hands of her enemies, and cruelly burned to death as a witch—declaring with her dying voice that she was sent from God—such was the "delegated maiden" whose name liveth evermore in the annals of France.

Joan of Arc was the personification of patriotism, one of the sublimest forms of devotion of which the soul is capable. The love of country is the life of a nation as

much as family love is the life of a household. Hence
the patriot is the focus of all that contributes to the existence and welfare of the nation, and takes highest rank
among the great men and women cherished in the memory of a people. The appreciation of this immortal virtue
is cosmopolitan, unconfined by limits of time, independent
even of the influences of civilisation. The deep and
universal admiration excited by the display of pure and
disinterested love of country is heightened by the odium
attaching to its counterpart. The term "traitor" is ever
bestowed and received with loathing; and while such
names as Curtius, Tell, and Garibaldi will never cease to
be encircled with a halo of glory, those of Judas, and
such as he, have become the synonyms of shame and contempt.

Joan of Arc is not, however, the only female who may
fearlessly claim the title of heroine. Indeed, the soul of
woman contains latent all that constitutes true heroism.
In social and domestic life it is so much a matter of constant observation, that it almost ceases to excite surprise
to see the shrinking and diffident woman become by force
of circumstances masculine in fortitude, forethought, and
understanding. Ever and anon in public life this truth
is illustrated and maintained; and as if to show that there
is no limit to this power of development, History records
the deeds of a Judith, a Charlotte Corday, and a Maid
of Saragossa, proofs, if need be, that woman can

"Stalk with Minerva's steps where Mars would quake to tread."

In the following pages we have attempted to delineate
one of these characters. And since opinions vary as to
whether the Maid of Orleans was a fanatic, or an adventurer lucky by a fortuitous concourse of circumstances,
or a divinely commissioned agent, a statement of facts

with the inferences deducible will help to form a fairly correct estimate of her character.

The record of the Maid of Orleans divides itself naturally into three periods :

1st. From her birth to the deliverance of Orleans.

2d. From the relief of Orleans to her capture at Compiègne.

3d. Her imprisonment, trial, and death at Rouen.

The authorities mainly relied on for the historical facts are: "Collection Complète des Memoires," Petitot, vol. viii.; "Le Livre de la Pucell," Le Roux; "Histoire do France," Mezeray; "Le Procès, etc.," Quicherat; "Histoire de France," Michaud and Michelet.

I.

THE PREPARATION.

" Look on thy country; look on fertile France
And see the cities and the towns defaced
By wasting ruin of the cruel foe."—SHAKESPEARE.

JOAN OF ARC, or more properly Jeanne Darc, was born about the year 1410, A.D. Her father was a peasant named James Darc, living at Domremy,* a village on the borders of that Lorraine which has recently been wrested from the French by the victorious Germans. Her mother's name was Isabella Romée, this latter word being a provincialism applied to those who had taken part in a pilgrimage to Rome to visit the tombs of the martyrs. Joan had three brothers, John, James, and Peter, and one sister.† She was the youngest of

* Anciently a fief or domaine of St Remy of Rheims.
† Michaud.

the family, which was supported by the labour of the
father, who cultivated his own patrimony.

The monarchy of France seemed at this epoch to be
tottering to its fall, and to be involving in its ruin the
kingdom itself. Charles VII. was king only in name.
The English were in possession of the northern and
western provinces from Calais to Bordeaux, and were
also masters of Rouen and Paris.

After the battle of Agincourt our own Henry V. had
espoused the daughter of the French king (Charles VI.),
and had been acknowledged heir to the French crown.
Had the life of Henry been spared, the two kingdoms of
England and France would probably have been united
under one sovereign, and England might have sunk into
a mere French province. The premature death of Henry
frustrated this, but his claims devolved upon his infant
son, in whose name the conquered provinces were held
by the Duke of Bedford, who had been appointed Regent of France.

On the death of Charles VI., A.D. 1393, his son, the
Dauphin, asserted his claim to the crown. His prospects
were disheartening in the extreme. The kingdom was
torn by anarchy, split into factions, half possessed by
foreigners, and distracted by civil war. The Duke of
Burgundy, although a vassal of the French king, was in
arms against his Suzerain, and the royal court was the seat
of faction, intrigue, and immorality. The character of the
queen mother (Isabella) was so scandalous, that doubts ex-
isted as to the legitimacy of the Dauphin, and loyalty itself
staggered under these suspicions. "Thus," says Lamartine,
"the king sought in vain his subjects among his people, the
people sought in vain their kingdom in the monarchy,
and the French sought in vain a country in France."

Such was the state of affairs when the child was born,

who was destined to become the political luminary and
salvation of her people. It is said that a prophecy had
been circulated in her native province, that deliverance
would spring from a maiden of Lorraine,* and although
this, doubtless, had primary reference to the marriage of
René of Anjou with the heiress of Lorraine, it was soon
to be indissolubly connected with our heroine.

Jeanne was tenderly beloved of her parents, and was
brought up by her mother in a domestic and useful
manner. It is true she was taught neither to read nor
to write, but in all the social duties of a labourer's
cottage she was well instructed. She became skilful
with her needle, and the happy hours of childhood were
spent at her mother's side learning the details of a
housewife's duties, and listening to those legends which
are always current among a people of lively imagination.

The family of Darc, though poor, was evidently pious.
The children bore three apostolic names, and the con-
nection of the mother's name with *pilgrimages* is a
further confirmation. Jeanne, with her active fancy,
never tired of hearing narrations, which, interesting in
themselves, derive additional charm from the mouth of
those we love. The lives of the saints, the legends of
the Church, incidents connected with pilgrimages,
memoirs of the martyrs, and such biblical knowledge as
might have been acquired in those days, were heard
again and again with pleasure, which was not diminished
by their repetition. No lessons make a deeper impression than those derived from a mother's lips, the instruc-
tion may not be systematic, or even accurate, but it will
never be effaced.

The native province of Jeanne was subjected, in its
turn, to the ravages of civil war. On one occasion the

* "Une Pucelle des Marches de Lorraine doit sauver le royaume."

family had to flee to the forest as a refuge from the
armed bands that were desolating the place.   Returning,
they found the greater part of the village in flames.
Incidents such as these could not but powerfully affect
the mind of one who had already begun to evince strong
liking for silent meditation and solitude.   Beautiful and
well-proportioned, she showed no desire to participate in
the amusements or frivolities of youth.   She loved to
attend the services of the Church, to retire for private
prayer, to carry her needlework into an enclosure behind
the house, whence she could see only the clear blue sky
above, the old tower of the village church, and the tops
of the distant mountains.   In these secret soul-commun-
ings she experienced that exalted pleasure which the
wise and good in all ages have professed to find in volun-
tary withdrawal from the tumult of the world, and in
meditations in which they seem to stand upon the thresh-
old of the Infinite.

These peculiarities of Jeanne's character did not escape
the observation of her parents.   They gently remonstrated
with her regarding her seclusion, her over fondness for the
Church services, and her frequent reveries; but it was
impossible to be angry with a child whose every look
was love, and every motion obedience.   Her mother,
from whose tales of the mysterious and the marvellous
she had imbibed the enthusiasm which is created by
such narrations, could alone sympathise with her, or
understand her feelings.

It is not surprising that a girl of such beauty, modesty,
piety, and tenderness, should have been an object of
admiration and attraction to the young men of the
village.   Many offers of marriage were made, and the
good offices of her parents on their behalf solicited.   She
resolved to remain free, as if taking for exemplars the

daughter of Jephthah and "the Blessed Mary, ever a virgin." It is related that one of her admirers, carried away by the force of his passions, demanded her as a matter of right, declaring upon his solemn oath before the magistrate that she had pledged her faith to him. This proved a turning-point in her career. It was not expected that the meek, silent, and retiring girl would think of resistance, but that she would allow judgment to go by default. Great was the astonishment, therefore, when she appeared before the judges, and, with much emotion, denied upon oath the calumny of the pretender. Judgment was given in her favour, and she returned home to be, as Lamartine observes, "the mother, not of a family, but of a kingdom."

II.

THE MANIFESTATION.

"God's mother deigned to appear to me,
  Will'd me to leave my base vocation,
  And free my country from calamity."—SHAKESPEARE.

"ARISE, Jeanne, go to the aid of the Dauphin—restore him his kingdom of France!"

Such was the mandate which Jeanne, at thirteen years of age, solemnly asserted she had heard in the churchyard of Domremy.

She had heard voices and seen visions before; they had recommended to her piety and virginity; they had demanded her pity for France and its miserable people. She had never spoken of these appearances and revelations, but they were the constant source of her anxious cogitations. It is open to question whence came these

visions and voices. We cannot suppose for a moment
that Jeanne was guilty of wilful or designing fraud in
attesting their reality. She had brooded over the
calamities of her nation, her heart had melted with pity
for the young Dauphin, fatherless, motherless, crownless.
In him was personified her country and its misfortunes;
for him her unceasing prayers were made to the
Almighty. Is it to be wondered at that at last all she
had heard, and thought, and prayed for was so powerfully concentred in her mind that hope became trans-
formed into faith, and that she heard with her outward
ears those internal voices which never ceased to speak?
"It is difficult for a man, and still more so for women,
when they are prepossessed passionately with an idea or a
doubt, when they question themselves, and listen within,
to distinguish between their own voice and voices from
heaven, and to be able to say this is from me, this is
from God. In such a condition man becomes his own
oracle, and takes his enthusiasm for divinity. The
wisest of men have been thus deceived as well as the
weakest women. History is full of these prodigies."
Plutarch tells us that Numa, after being elected King of
Rome, in order to obtain greater reverence for his laws,
declared that he held frequent intercourse with a goddess
who inspired him with wisdom and understanding.*
Socrates never ceased to profess himself guided by an
internal voice, to which he paid implicit obedience, and
on which he relied for counsel in cases of difficulty.
When this silent monitor left him he felt that his career
was ended. Even the great Napoleon, whom no one
will accuse of superstitious weakness, was subject to this
mysterious influence. On the eve of his celebrated invasion of Russia, when the tension of his mind must

---

* Plutarch, vol. l., p. 166.

have been extreme, he frequently thought he heard a voice calling him by name, and so audibly that he would leave his apartment, inquiring, "Who called me?" *

Why should less credit be given to the avowals in this respect of a young and unsophisticated village maiden, whose whole life was an exemplification of sincerity and truth, who never ceased to appeal to "the voices," and who died attesting their reality, than has been given to more exalted personages? She had been nourished with legends and tales of prodigies, of fairies, saints and angels, of visions, and dreams, and revelations. She believed them possible, she believed them accomplished. Her faith was as candid and sincere as it was unselfish, and it supplied a motive power to excite as well as an index to guide in the discharge of the dangerous duties of a devoted patriotism.

Her first vision caused her great alarm, but others succeeded. She saw St Michael in celestial armour. She had seen him times innumerable in the altarpiece of the village church. She saw St Margaret and St Catherine, the popular saints of the country. They were crowned with sparkling diadems and attended by angels. They spoke to her in accents of unearthly sweetness, deploring the misery of the kingdom, and engaging her sympathy. When the voices ceased, and the vision was over, Jeanne was desolate and in tears. We can imagine her in the attitude in which Milton describes Adam after an angelic conference :

> " The angel ended, and in Adam's ear
> So charming left his voice, that he awhile
> Thought him still speaking, still stood fixed to hear."

" I could have wished," said Jeanne, in the agony of

* Segur's "Invasion of Russia."

her last trial, "that those angels had carried me away with them."

For several years this phantasy lasted, and at length silence became insupportable. Her terrible mission became more clearly revealed, and the supernatural summons to discharge it, more imperative. She made her mother her confidant. The mother is the natural receptacle of family secrets, and happy are the children who have a resource in this fountain of perennial affection. At first the disclosure was received with incredulity, but its persistence commanded attention, and from being the subject of sarcasm became the staple topic of the family gossip.

The father of Jeanne, however, was not a sentimentalist. Plain, honest, and sincere, he was neither credulous nor enthusiastic. He could believe implicitly the noble story of Deborah, and the scarcely less noble account of Judith, for these had the sanction of the Church. But that such things could happen in his own day, in his native village, in his own family, was a notion to be scouted and put down. He told Jeanne without reserve, and in no tender accents, that rather than see her mixing with soldiers and attending the camp, he would order her brothers to drown her as they would a kitten, nay, that he would drown her with his own hands.

Jeanne's position was now one of the most difficult and painful character. Disobedience of some kind seemed inevitable. If she gave up all thought of saving her country she rejected the mission to which Heaven had called her. If she endeavoured to fulfil that behest she disobeyed her parents, and broke the fifth commandment. She wrought a way out of this dilemma with prayers and tears. Ignorant, perhaps, of the history of

Elisha, she must have experienced his feelings when he said, " Let me first kiss my father and mother, and then I will follow thee."

Like Cromwell, in after-times she might have wished that the Lord would not lay this burden upon her. Who has not experienced the anguish of that supreme hour when some irrevocable and all-important step must be taken which may make or mar the fortune of a life. The crisis came. The call of duty gave no uncertain sound, and was responded to by no infirmity of purpose. All considerations of self were extinguished, and the deep resolution was taken to sacrifice, if need were, parents, relations, the paternal house, the native village, the dear friends of youth, and even life itself, at the shrine of duty.

III.

THE MISSION ACCEPTED.

" Skill to direct, and strength to strike the blow,
To manage with address, to seize with power,
The crisis of a dark decisive hour."—COWPER.

To escape the displeasure and severity which she had reason to fear on the part of her parents, Jeanne repaired to the house of her uncle, André Laxart. She found there a welcome and a home. But the charge which she felt she had received from Heaven was never absent from her thoughts. She laid the matter unreservedly before her uncle, and begged his guidance and assistance. More credulous, and perhaps more indulgent, than her father, he so far complied with her wishes as to go to Count Baudricourt, the governor of Vaucouleurs, a garrison town in the vicinity of Domremy, and relate to him

the history of his niece, and the object she had in view.
One hardly knows which to admire most, the honest
simplicity of the uncle going on such an errand, or the
courtesy of a military officer listening to what must have
seemed to him utter absurdity.   That a peasant girl of
seventeen should offer to do what statesmen and cavaliers
could not do, to restore a kingdom which seemed in the
throes of dissolution, must have sounded to the veteran
warrior "like a tale told by an idiot."

He dismissed the good-natured uncle, who felt somewhat abashed under the governor's derision, with this
piece of advice, "Box her ears, and send her back to her
father."

Irresolution is often the result rather of infirmity of
mind than want of principle.   As the rush bends before
the breeze in any direction, so the man who does not
clearly perceive the course to be taken becomes passive,
and is swayed almost unresistingly by the stronger in-
tellect which can decide quickly and act promptly.
Jeanne's uncle returned home wondering that he could
have believed in her pretensions.   In her presence he
had caught something of her honest enthusiasm, in the
interview with the matter-of-fact Baudricourt, that enthusiasm had evaporated; but, returned home, he was
again within the magic circle of his niece's influence.
The character of the heroine now becomes marked.   She
was not daunted by difficulties, and the chilling reception
which her uncle had experienced did not damp her
ardour.   When told that the governor laughed at the
idea of her assisting the Dauphin, she begged to be conducted to him that she might plead her cause in person.
After some hesitation this was acceded to, and Jeanne
left her native village never to return.

In company with her uncle she set out in the dress of a

peasant girl, and proceeded to Vaucouleurs on foot. She had resolved to avoid the pain of parting from relatives and friends by informing nobody of her intention. Yet her thoughts often reverted to the loved ones, and many a lingering look behind was given on the journey. Kindred natures with hers can alone appreciate the poignancy of the sacrifice which the warm-hearted and tender girl was now making, and it is difficult to understand what other principle than a keen sense of duty could have carried her onwards.

Having arrived at Vaucouleurs she lodged at the house of a cousin, and her uncle repaired once more to the governor, who was amazed at this perseverance. After some hesitation he granted the interview as the only way of getting rid of this troublesome subject. He was greatly impressed with the beauty and modesty of the young peasant girl, who, having never before left her native village, nor ever associated with any above her own station, conducted herself with the utmost propriety and even dignity.

"Why have you wished to see me?" said he.

"My lord," said Jeanne, "I come to you in the name of God, in order that you may direct the Dauphin to remain where he is at present, and by no means to give battle to the enemy, for God will give him succour in Mid-Lent."

"But the Dauphin is master of his own actions, and may not care to receive advice from me."

"The kingdom," replied Jeanne, "does not belong to him, but to God his Sovereign, who has destined the kingdom for him; and in spite of his enemies he shall be king, and I am appointed to conduct him to his coronation at Rheims."

The governor listened with astonishment. The matter

appeared too serious to be summarily dismissed. He
said he would think it over, and the interview was
brought to a close. His position was difficult, since it
seemed impossible to avoid, on the one hand, the reproach
of infidelity, or on the other the stigma of superstition.
He consulted the clergy, and it was resolved that the
governor and the curé of Vaucouleurs should together
visit the Maiden at her cousin's house, and examine her
minutely as to her pretensions. This was done with all
solemnity, the priest in his sacerdotal robes and the governor attended by his officers. The priestly vestments were
considered a defence against evil spirits, for clergy as well
as laity were only too ready to impute everything extraordinary to diabolical influence. As a preliminary, Jeanne
was exorcised. The curé first made the sign of the cross
upon her, made her kneel down, and sprinkled her with
holy water. He then recited some litanies, psalms, and
prayers. Then he asked the (supposed) demon his name,
and adjured him by Christ to come out and enter into
her no more. Laying his right hand upon her head, he
repeated the formula officially prescribed for such occasions, "I exorcise thee, thou unclean spirit, in the name
of Jesus Christ. Tremble, O Satan, thou enemy of the
faith, foe of mankind, who hast brought death into the
world, deprived men of life, and rebelled against justice.
Thou seducer of mankind, fruit of evil, source of avarice,
discord, and envy, avaunt!"

Jeanne passed through this terrible ordeal satisfactorily.
It was evident she was not possessed by evil spirits, and
her artless simplicity and almost superhuman faith
silenced all objections, if they did not induce conviction.
The priest and the governor were deeply impressed, and
withdrew without coming to any decision.

These transactions soon gave rise to considerable ex-

citement in the town. All classes were interested in a
subject which touched their curiosity, their faith, and
their patriotism. The female portion of the community
especially took the matter up, and it is well known that
their influence is by no means insignificant.   Some
ardently espoused the cause, and even those who doubted
could not but wish well to the noble-hearted girl.   Some
one having said to her, "Well, it seems the king must
be driven away, and we shall all become English;" she
replied, "It is necessary that before Mid-Lent I should
see the Dauphin. If I go to him on my knees I must
go, for no one else can retake the kingdom of France. I
would indeed rather remain with my poor mother," she
added sadly, "for I know that fighting is not my trade,
but I must go and do what my Sovereign commands me."
Being asked to whom she was referring, she replied that
God was her Sovereign, whom she was bound to obey.
These words were not lost. Among those who were
listening to her were two cavaliers.   They were so
deeply touched that they pledged their knightly honour
to bring her, if it were within the bounds of possibility,
into the presence of the Dauphin.

Baudricourt at last resolved to place the matter before
his superior, the Duke of Lorraine, and thus relieve
himself of responsibility.   The duke resolved to put
the Maiden at once to a practical test. He desired a
miracle, which he thought was a necessary sign in a
person directly commissioned. Human nature, unless it
sees signs and wonders, will not believe, and yet by a
strange perversity even such evidence is not always submitted to. The duke consulted her about his own health,
and seemed desirous that she should relieve him of a
malady under which he was suffering. Jeanne spoke
only of a moral disease; she advised him to benefit his

soul by ceasing to live in hatred and estrangement from
his wife. We are not told by what means Jeanne became acquainted with the duke's private affairs, yet we
cannot but admire the moral courage with which she
gave wholesome but perhaps unpalatable advice. Jeanne
returned to Vaucouleurs, having apparently effected nothing by this visit.

In the meantime, communications had been opened
with the Dauphin, it is supposed by Baudricourt. Representations coming from such a quarter received that
attention which would not have been otherwise obtained.
Again the cause of Jeanne was espoused by her own sex,
the ladies of the Court, and especially the mother-in-law
of the Dauphin, Yolande of Sicily, thought that at least
an opportunity should be afforded of putting these extraordinary pretensions to the proof. The Dauphin, having
no inherent strength of character, was irresolute, but his
cause was desperate—the siege of Orleans was being
pressed vigorously by the English, its fate seemed hopeless, and with Orleans would fall the last bulwark of
resistance to the flood of invasion. By availing himself
of whatever influence might spring from the circumstance
of a young and beautiful maiden claiming to be sent from
God, and leading troops to battle, he might gain some
advantage, but could lose nothing. It was determined
to see her, and to test her capabilities.

The Court was then at Chinon, near Tours, whither
Jeanne was invited to proceed.

The news of her intended departure soon spread
through Vaucouleurs, and reached the little village of
Domremy. Her family, who believed her to be crazy,
hastened to the town to remonstrate, and if possible to
restrain her. She listened with humility to their en-
treaties, and mingled her tears with theirs, but the

weakness of the woman could not soften the resolution
of the heroine; the distress of her country outweighed
altogether, in her estimation, the grief of a family.   The
inhabitants of Vaucouleurs purchased for her a horse
and also a soldier's dress, which was as much a protection for her person as a sign of her mission as a champion.
Baudricourt gave her a sword.   As she mounted her
horse to depart, the governor playfully asked her if she
intended ever to come back, and settle quietly down as
a good little wife.   She replied, "Nay, nay, it is not yet
time to speak of wedded life and peaceful rest.   But the
Lord will provide."

Jeanne was escorted by two gentlemen who had
solemnly pledged themselves for her safety, and by some
mounted horsemen engaged for this service.   She left
Vaucouleurs amid the acclamations of its people, her face
beaming with satisfaction at this public recognition of
her character and the approaching accomplishment of her
purpose.   The journey was a dangerous one, for it lay
450 miles through provinces then under the power of the
Burgundians or of the English.   Jeanne and her escort
travelled chiefly by night for greater safety, sleeping
when and where they could.   Sometimes they bivouacked
on the ground, Jeanne being wrapped in a warm woollen
coverlet, and always retaining her soldier's dress.   And
as a man's foes are as often in his own connections as
from without, Jeanne had more to fear from friends than
from open enemies.   By her escort she was regarded
with mixed feelings of incredulity and superstition.
Sometimes they thought her a saint and sometimes a
sorceress; now they were ready to worship her, and
anon took counsel to destroy her.   On one occasion they
had almost determined to hurl her into a mountain torrent, and report that the devil had flown away with her.

But a mysterious influence surrounded "The Maid," and treason

> " Could but peep to what it would
> Acted little of its will."

On the 6th March Jeanne arrived safely at Chinon after a journey of eleven days, and was received with every mark of respect at the castle of Count Goncourt, in the neighbourhood.

IV.

THE ROYAL ASSENT.

" Go, and the Lord be with thee."—SAUL.

CHARLES, although he had promised to receive the peasant girl, and listen to her statement, seemed unwilling to redeem his word. He took counsel with many, and followed the advice of none. Sometimes inspired with manly resolution, and sometimes immersed in the lap of pleasure, his affairs were at a crisis, with which his youth and inexperience were unable to cope. Jeanne was visited by the queen and the ladies of the Court; they were charmed with her modesty and enthusiasm, and they reported very favourably of her to the Dauphin. They urged her reception, and Charles at length yielded.

It is highly probable that the urgent representations which had been received from Dunois, the gallant defender of Orleans, as to the impossibility of the city holding out, had the greatest influence upon the Court. " Let her come, the Maid from the forests of Lorraine; let her come in the name of God, and deliver them if God willed, for except in Him, the city had no hope."

On the 9th March Jeanne received a message from the

Dauphin that he would grant her an interview. Attired in her peasant dress, she was conducted by Louis de Bourbon into the royal presence. The numerous attendance of councillors, courtiers, and the usual retinue of a Court, evinced the interest which the subject had excited. The Dauphin had designedly disguised himself in order to test the pretended inspiration. If she comes from God, said he, she will infallibly detect the heir to the crown, even though disguised and mingled with the crowd; but if her inspiration be demoniacal, she will assuredly choose by outward appearances. Such reasoning was indeed feeble and inconclusive, but men often satisfy themselves with arguments quite as shallow.

Jeanne entered abashed, confused, and apparently dazzled with the splendour and state of the assembled Court. Looking timidly around, she seemed to be searching for the particular individual to whom she was sent. Amid profound silence she recognised the prince, and approaching him modestly, but without hesitation, she fell upon her knees before him. The prince pretended that she was mistaken, but she replied emphatically that it was not so, and in clear and solemn tones she addressed him thus—

"Most noble Dauphin, the King of Heaven commands you, through me, to proceed to the city of Rheims, there to be consecrated and crowned, and to be His lieutenant of the kingdom of France."

Astonishment and derision pervaded the Court. There seemed then as much probability of Charles being crowned at Rheims as of making a journey to the moon. But the Dauphin was deeply impressed with the language and demeanour of the Maid, and taking her aside, he inquired of her concerning a secret which had distressed and disturbed him greatly, and had often damped his ardour. We have already alluded to the scandalous conduct of the queen mother, and the suspicions to which it gave rise. Charles had never spoken of this terrible secret to any one, but, like a canker, it was corroding his peace of mind.* Jeanne's answer was most assuring. Bending before him with reverence, she said, with an audible voice—"I tell thee, on the part of God, that thou art the true son of the king, and rightful heir of France."

The satisfaction which beamed from the face of the Dauphin was reflected from the Court. The mysterious messenger had espoused the falling cause with superhuman ardour. In her were enlisted, for the Dauphin's sake, religion, mystery, chivalry, beauty, patriotism. Henceforth doubt and lukewarmness would partake of the nature of treason, for God's ambassador had solemnly pronounced in favour of Charles's legitimacy and rights. The enthusiasm which had gushed forth at Vaucouleurs was percolating at Chinon. The Court was inclined, and the people were clamorous, to give the Maid of Lorraine an opportunity to exhibit practically the power with which she claimed to be invested by the express commission of the Almighty.

Charles, however, could not altogether break away from the grave and cautious representations of statesmen who had grown grey in the service of the State, and who looked upon all enthusiasm as youthful indiscretion. Although with regard to the mission of the Maid they could not deny that " there was something in it," yet they thought that proof sufficient of her character and inspiration had not been offered to warrant them in com-

---

* Souvent il entroit dans son Oratorie où la face contre terre et toute baignée de pleurs il prioit ardemment Sa Divine Majesté do montrer s'il etait legitime heritier du Royaume."—MEZERAY.

mitting the destiny of the kingdom into her hands. Moreover, in those days the last appeal lay to the pope, and either directly or indirectly the sanction of the Church was necessary to equip completely a person or a project. After some hesitation, it was resolved to send the Maid to Poitiers, there to be examined before the Parliament and the University, which bodies being driven from Paris, were then holding their sessions in that provincial city.

When this decision was communicated to Jeanne, she exclaimed—"Ah, well, I see I shall have a stern trial at Poitiers, but God will assist me. Let us therefore proceed with confidence." Accordingly, Jeanne duly appeared before this grave and venerable assembly. To the abstruse questions of learned professors, or the common sense objections of practical politicians, she had nothing to offer but the confession of a simple faith. God had called her to the work of saving France, and would help her to do it in His own way.

One of her examiners said—"If God has decided to save France, he has no need of men-at-arms." The objection, ignoring as it does the fact that God works by means, was scarcely deserving a reply, but Jeanne was prepared for it. She answered—"The men-at-arms must fight, and God will give the victory."

As the visions at Domremy evidently formed the source and sustenance of her faith, great efforts were made to dispel her belief in these by texts and quotations tending to show that the age of direct divine revelation had passed away, and that, therefore, visions and voices were incredible. "That may be," said she, "but there are more things written in the Book of God than in the books of men."

A councillor, who spoke French with idiomatic inaccuracy, having asked her somewhat sneeringly—" Did the voices speak good French," Jeanne answered somewhat sharply—" Better than you speak." On it being remarked to her that if she gave no better proof of her divine credentials than mere assertion, the king would not entrust his soldiers to her command. Jeanne exclaimed—" God is my witness that I am not sent to give signs at Poitiers. Send me to Orleans with troops, many or few as you please, and there I will give one. The sign that I give is this—The siege of Orleans shall be raised."

The council separated and reported to the king:

1. That they found nothing in the Maid of Lorraine unbecoming a good Catholic.

2. That nothing was impossible with God.

3. That the Bible furnished examples, which might be quoted as authorising a woman to fight in manly attire for the deliverance of her country.

To this testimony was added a report, after personal examination by the queen, Yolande of Sicily, the Dauphin's mother-in-law, and a committee of matrons, attesting the virginity of the Maiden. There was no longer ground for irresolution, and the following proclamation was issued by royal command:

" The king, seeing the necessity of his kingdom, ought not to reject the Maid who declares she is sent of God to succour him. Following Holy Writ, he has sought to prove her in two ways: (1.) By human prudence inquiring into her life and behaviour. (2.) By devout prayer, asking a sign whether she be come by the will of God or no. The king has accordingly kept her near to him for six weeks, and has caused her birth, life, conduct, and intentions to be inquired into by all manner of people, who have publicly and privately conversed with her, and will find in her not any evil, but only

chastity, humility, devotion, simplicity, and honour; and
many marvellous things are told of her birth and life.

"The king has received a sign from her, for she says
that before the city of Orleans she will show him a sign
and not elsewhere, for so God has commanded her.

"Therefore, having regard to this, that no harm is found
in her, that she promises a sign before Orleans, that she is
constant in her purpose, and urgently pleads that she may
go to Orleans with men-at-arms, the king ought not to hold
her back, but to let her go thither honourably, trusting
in God, since to doubt her or to set her aside would be
to render himself unworthy of the succour of God."

This proclamation was received with universal satisfaction, and no efforts were spared to send her forth
suitably equipped. A suit of armour of spotless white,
symbolising her purity, was prepared for her, and a
noble black charger was provided for her use. Several
officers of the king's retinue had given her daily training
in the management of her steed, and in the use of the
lance, in both of which exercises she soon acquired considerable skill. She had requested to be furnished with
a mysterious sword, marked with five crosses, which she
declared "the Voices" had informed her was buried
behind the altar of a neighbouring church. They sent
and found it in the place described, and a scabbard of
crimson velvet was provided for it; but Jeanne preferred
a scabbard of leather. With the sword at her side also
hung a small battle-axe. She wore no helmet, desiring
no other covering for her head than her own beautiful
amber hair.' In her hand she carried a banner of white
satin, bearing the names Jesus and Maria, and embroid-
ered with white lilies, the heraldic flower of France.
Thus she set out, attended by her tried protector and
friend, Daulon, a brave old cavalier; two little boys,

her pages; two heralds-at-arms, a chaplain, a suite of attendants, and an immense concourse of people, who were almost ready to worship, not only her, but even the horse she sat on. She met with a most enthusiastic reception at Blois; both soldiers and people felt and submitted to the influences which her character created. Jeanne began by reforming the abuses which prevailed among the soldiery, rightly judging that brutality and profligacy as much destroyed their discipline as it rendered them unworthy of Divine assistance. Cards and dice were thrown to the flames, gambling of every kind forbidden, and oaths and indecent language punished. She insisted that officers and men should attend the public services of the Church. Popular preachers attested the divinity of her mission, altars were erected in public places, and the sacrament administered. Earnest and incessant appeals to the strongest feelings of our nature, love, patriotism, pity, religion, could not but excite like a tempest the minds of the people. The army felt the power of pure and holy influences, and became animated by impulses similar to those which sustained the Crusaders who marched to glory and to victory less by the lightning flash of their swords and of their battle-axes, than by the thunder cry which was at once their warrant and their watchword, " God wills it."

V.

THE DELIVERANCE.

" A holy maid hither with me I bring,
Which, by a vision sent to her from heaven,
Ordained us to raise this tedious siege."—SHAKESPEARE.

THE English, under the Earl of Salisbury, had laid siege to Orleans, 12th October 1428. The inhabitants of that

city, loyal to their sovereign, made a determined and
heroic resistance; for they knew well that the fall of
Orleans involved the ruin of the French monarchy.
The English pressed forward their earthworks, and thus
advanced nearer and nearer to the city, connecting their
forts, of which they had about sixty, and completely
investing the city on the north.

" On the south, Orleans was connected with the north
bank of the Loire by a strong fortified bridge, defended
by two towers called the Tourelles, built on the bridge
itself, just at the point where it rested on a little island.
The stonework of the bridge terminated at these Tourelles, and a drawbridge extended thence to the southern
shore. At the head of the bridge was a small fort or
tête du pont, and this, in conjunction with the Tourelles,
created a really formidable outwork capable of holding a
large garrison, and enabling its citizens to go out under its
shelter and obtain supplies and reinforcements from the
southern provinces."

It is evident, therefore, that the possession of these
Tourelles was an important matter, and accordingly the
Earl of Salisbury spared no efforts for their acquisition.
After several attacks, he carried them by assault, 23d
October 1428. The doom of the city now appeared
certain, but from this moment the tide of victory turned.
The earl having ascended one of the Tourelles to survey
the town, was struck by a stone shot from the city, and
died within eight days. His successor in command was
inferior to him in ability; but still the city was exposed
to a merciless attack, and it was evident that its submission was only a question of time.

Resistance, however, was prolonged through the
winter, although famine was beginning to be felt in the
beleaguered city. But in March 1629, Sir John Fastolfe

gained a decisive victory over the French at Rouvrai, near Orleans, and by thus clearing the surrounding country of the French and their Scottish allies, enabled large convoys of food and ammunition to reach in safety the English camp. This is called the battle of the Herrings, because large supplies of salt fish were thus enabled to reach the army. The English, elated with their victory and their supplies, were in high spirits, while the people of Orleans were proportionately depressed, and even Dunois, who held the city, felt that he could not much longer defer the fatal hour of surrender.

It was under these circumstances that the Maid of Lorraine set out from Blois to go to the relief of Orleans. She had requested to be conducted by the shortest route, but the French officers, fearing they might fall in with some of the English bands, preferred the longer and safer course. When they arrived in sight of the city, Jeanne was mortified to find that she had been deceived, and that the river ran between her and the city she desired to enter. Dunois, as soon as he perceived her from the ramparts, crossed the river in a small boat, and approached her with respectful salutations.

"Are you," said she, "the bastard of Orleans?"

"Yes," he replied, "and right glad am I to see you."

"Have you then," she said reproachfully, "counselled to bring me the longest way, for fear of the enemy?"

"It was the advice of the best and bravest officers," said Dunois.

"My lord," replied Jeanne, "the counsel of God is better than yours. Do not fear for me. God prepares my way, and will accomplish that for which I was born. I bring you the best succour that ever cavalier or city received—the help of God."

During this interview the storm which agitated the

Loire, and had prevented the flotilla of supply from entering the port of Orleans, subsided, and the city was revictualled in spite of the English.

The next day (29th April 1429), having sent back the escort which had been provided for her by the king, she entered Orleans at the head of only two hundred lances. It is difficult to understand why the English made no attempt to dispute her passage, which they could easily have prevented, but it is probable they felt sure of capturing the city, and were lulled by over-confidence. Jeanne, mounted on a white steed, clad in her shining armour, and carrying in her right hand the beautiful banner, passed through the streets of the town. She seemed at once the angel of war and peace, and the enthusiasm of the populace knew no bounds. Priests and people, soldiers, women, and children, all pressed round her, anxious, if possible, to touch her, believing that a celestial virtue emanated from her. She proceeded to the church, where a *Te Deum* was chanted; for confidence in the Divine protection and a feeling of entire security pervaded all ranks. The presence of the Maid, like that of Napoleon in after-times, was as good as a reinforcement of 10,000 men.

When the entry of the "Maiden from Lorraine" into the city, with troops and provisions, was fully known to the English, they were not a little disquieted. The audacity and genius which had enabled her to break through their lines were attributed to Satan. The remarkable egotism which induces, according to a modern French writer, the English to believe that the Saviour of the world only died for the English, was not unknown in those days. Every victory achieved by them was regarded as a proof of the Divine goodwill, and that God would send a messenger to take the part of their foes was utterly inconceivable. The woman, they thought, must be a witch, an object of the grossest terror and superstition in that age of credulity; and stout hearts that had never quailed amid the roar of the battle-field, melted before a phantom of their own creation.

Jeanne lost no time in attempting the relief of the city, and dictated the following letter to the English commanders:

"King of England, and you, Duke of Bedford, who call yourself the Regent of France, and you, William, Earl of Suffolk, John Talbot, and you, Thomas Scales, who pretend to be the lieutenant of Bedford, obey the King of Heaven, restore the keys of this kingdom to the Maiden sent from God! And you, archers and men-at-arms before Orleans, return, in God's name, to your own country! O King of England, if you do not obey, I am chief of the war, and whenever I reach you, be assured I will punish you. The King of Heaven will send me more power than you will be able to bring against me. But if you will make peace we are ready to treat with you, and will gladly welcome you as allies and friends."

This important document was carried to the English lines by one of her heralds. It was received with mingled feelings of derision and rage; Goliath's reception of the stripling David could hardly have been more contemptuous. This was hardly to be wondered at; but the treatment accorded to the herald was in utter defiance of the rules of etiquette or chivalry. He was put into fetters and imprisoned, and so remained till the siege was raised. Jeanne, nothing disheartened, mounted the ramparts near the Tourelles, and repeated aloud her message. This post was held by Sir William Gladsdale, a rude and boisterous captain, who cared for nothing and nobody. He called her names of vulgarity, and told

her to go home and attend to her cows. She offered to
meet Talbot in single combat, and thus decide the issue
of the siege. Talbot did not consider the challenge
worthy a reply, but it afforded unlimited mirth and
derision to the English soldiery.

Jeanne, however, breathed nothing but war. She
was impatient at what was to her the over-caution of
experienced veterans, and which seemed a distrust of the
Divine assistance she had brought with her. On hearing
that a considerable reinforcement of English was approaching the city, she earnestly requested to be informed
as soon as they made their appearance, and this was
promised by the bastard of Orleans, who, if he did not
believe in her inspiration, was not insensible to the
enthusiasm which she excited in the troops and people.
Yet there were not wanting those who either distrusted
her pretensions or were jealous of her influence, and who,
though they pretended to defer to her advice, yet resolved,
if possible, to act without her. One old captain in particular grumbled thus: "Since they listen here more to
the advice of a plebeian adventurer than to an old soldier
like myself, I have nothing more to say. My sword
will speak for itself in the proper time and place. Honour, as well as the king's interests, forbid me to listen to
such nonsense. I shall strike my flag and become merely
a private soldier." A favourable occasion for making an
attack upon the English garrison having presented itself,
Dunois and his fellow knights led on their troops to the
assault. Jeanne was resting at home after the fatigues
of the morning undergone in her arduous efforts to re-
establish piety and discipline among the soldiers. Suddenly arousing herself, she called her faithful friend and
esquire (Daulon), and desired to be armed forthwith, for,
said she, "my heart tells me to go against the English."

Whilst being accoutred a great commotion was raised in the town. The report was raised that the French were repulsed, and were being slain at the very gates. "Alas, alas," said she, "why did you not wake me? The blood of Frenchmen is being spilt. To arms! to arms! My horse! my horse!"

Jeanne having mounted, her standard was handed to her from a window, and she galloped towards the gate of the city. On her way she encountered some of the wounded French. "Alas," said she, "I never see the blood of a Frenchman without my hair standing on end."

Dunois had attacked the Bastile de St Loup, but had been repulsed by the English under Talbot. Jeanne rallied the fugitives, brought up reinforcements, drove back the English, seized the bastile, and took the garrison prisoners. She wished to avoid the shedding of blood, and could not refrain from tears at the sight of the carnage. Having mounted a tower, she attached a letter to an arrow and shot it into the English camp. It was a second summons to surrender, and met with no better reception than the first. They sent back by the same method the most scurrilous answers and infamous reproaches. She blushed in reading them, but her conscious innocence soon restored her to equanimity. "God knows," she exclaimed, "that they are false."

Dunois advised a sortie and general assault, but was again repulsed. Jeanne was an anxious observer, and, seeing the retreat of the French, she sprang into a boat, leading by the bridle her horse, who swam across the river. She mounted and galloped into the thick of the fight. Her presence restored the spirits of the troops; they turned and renewed the combat with fury. The forts were taken, and Jeanne set fire to them with her own hand. She was wounded in the fight on this occasion by an arrow, but she declined to take food, having vowed to fast that day for the safety of her people.

Dunois thought that such unexpected success justified a truce, although it is probable he was overborne by the advice of some who were jealous of the success which had attended the Maid. The opinion of the council of war being reported to Jeanne, she replied, "No, you have been at your counsels and I at mine. Let the army be ready to-morrow, for I shall have more work yet to do." She charged her chaplain to wake her at break of day, and not to quit her, "for," said she, "blood will flow from my body; I shall be wounded."

The next day (7th May) having been aroused, she prepared to take the field. Her host tried to restrain her, and begged her to partake of some fish which had just been caught. She smiled, and requested him to put it by till the evening, "when I return," said she, "across the bridge in triumph." The captain who had charge of the gate refused to open it, but the infuriated multitude threatened to tear him in pieces, and he was forced to yield. The troops poured out like a torrent, and the officers were carried along with an impetuosity they could not withstand. Fiercely the attack was made upon the Tourelles, fiercely it was repulsed. The French fought with a tenacity which is not their usual characteristic, for, though they always charge with vivacity, they seem unable to sustain the impetus. But they believed themselves fighting under the shadow of the cross, led by an angel sent from God. Lance to lance, battle-axe to battle-axe, the combat was obstinately maintained. The carnage was fearful. Jeanne was the first to ascend the ladder, and reached the ramparts sword in hand. At this moment an arrow pierced her neck, and she fell into the trench. The English hastened to seize her body, which would have been an inestimable trophy, but her troops valiantly defended her, and she was carried in safety to the rear.

Great was the consternation excited by this incident in the minds of the French. To lose their heroine, their champion, their prophetess, was to lose all. They began to yield. Jeanne, smarting under the pain of her wound, could not refrain from tears—a proof at once of her weakness and womanhood. But, sensible how much depended on her presence, she rallied with an effort, snatched with her own hand the arrow from her flesh, and to those who wished to charm away the pain and evil effects of the wound she remarked, "I would rather die than sin against God."

Having anointed the wound with oil, she retired for private prayer. Then remounting, she returned to the fray, and urged a renewal of the attack. Dunois advised a retreat. "No," said she, "sound a halt, and let the troops eat and drink. The victory is yet within our reach."

The soldiers having refreshed themselves, Jeanne again advanced at their head, their champion and their inspiration. Her beautiful banner, recovered from the trench where she had fallen, was again placed in her hand. It floated in the breeze, and became in the sunshine a conspicuous object. The French redoubled their efforts. The English, seeing again "the monstrous woman," whom they had believed to be killed, were disconcerted. At this juncture the townspeople, who had been watching the contest, seized with enthusiasm, poured out of the gate, and attempted to cross the bridge in order to take part in the affray. They found one of the arches broken, but a plank was thrown across, and on they pressed. A panic seized the English. They could not understand either the impetuosity of the French or the apparent resurrection of "the Maid." Fear gave force to their imagination. They thought they saw celestial warriors fighting against them. They would fearlessly meet men, but they would not confront the supernatural. They gave way in spite of all that their captain, Gladsdale, could do to restrain them. "Advance, my children," said Jeanne to her troops, "at last we have them;" and the French swarmed over the wall and took possession of the ramparts.

Gladsdale and some thirty knights crossed the draw-bridge and retreated towards the Tourelles. "Yield thee, Glacidas," said Jeanne, "thou hast shamefully insulted me, but I pity thy soul and the souls of thy men."

At these words the bridge, struck by a cannon shot, gave way, and Gladsdale and his company were precipitated into the Loire. Jeanne could not refrain from tears at this terrible sight; but the battle was won. Not an Englishman was left on the south bank of the river Loire; those who were not killed were taken prisoners into Orleans.

Jeanne had promised to return in triumph across the bridge. The people resolved that this prediction should be literally accomplished. They set to work with energy, and in a short time the way was sufficiently repaired to enable her to cross. She entered Orleans amid the ringing of bells, the shouts of the soldiery, and the blessings of the people. The victory was due to her, but she ascribed it to God. The city was intoxicated with the joy of triumph. They would have worshipped her had she permitted it. To them she was their salvation, glory, and religion embodied, and he would have been roughly handled who at that time had dared to question her divinity.

She had redeemed her pledge, turned the tide of victory, hurled back the hitherto invincible English, saved the last prop of the French monarchy, and the shouts that resounded through the streets, "Glory to God and the Maid," testified to the gratitude and devotion of the liberated city. The battle had lasted from 10 A.M. till 9 P.M., and an ancient chronicler says: "The English lost 8000 or 9000 men, the French only 110 or 120, which shows clearly that it was the work of the Most High."

To commemorate this great achievement a huge crucifix was afterwards raised at the end of the bridge, on the right side of which was the statue of Charles VII. kneeling, and on the other side, in the same posture, the statue of her who is henceforth known as "The Maid of Orleans."

VI.

PROGRESS OF VICTORY.

" Down, down the wind she swims and sails away,
Now stoops upon it, and now grasps the prey."

THE following day the English acknowledged their defeat by raising the siege, which had lasted seven months. They retreated in good order, and appeared to offer battle in the plain. The French were strongly tempted to accept the challenge, but were restrained by the authority of the Maid. "No," said she, "let them go and let us be thankful for their departure."

In accordance with her express desire, a thanksgiving service was held in the cathedral. There were mingled in accents of praise the voices of priests and warriors, of women and children. Hearts swelled with gratitude for the joyful victory, and every eye was turned upon her who was at once its source and its symbol. After the service a solemn procession was made around the walls of the city.

But Jeanne well knew that no time was to be lost in festivities. She mounted her charger, and led her victorious troops to Blois. From thence she proceeded to Tours, and was received with every mark of respect and veneration by the Dauphin. She urged him to proceed forthwith to Rheims, there to be consecrated and crowned King of France. To carry out this suggestion seemed more impracticable than to raise the siege of Orleans. The country was overrun by the English and their allies, the Burgundians, and any attempt to reach Rheims would be met by a desperate resistance. Yet the advice was sound as well as daring. The invaders were likely to be discouraged after their unexpected and decisive defeat. They attributed to the Maid supernatural power, and superstition would unnerve their arm. Moreover, the young son of Henry V. had not been crowned, and if the Dauphin's coronation could be first accomplished, it would not fail to give him great advantages. But still his council demurred, and Charles was of too fickle a disposition to decide for himself between the sneers of some and the grave opinions of others. One day while they were deliberating, the Maid knocked gently at the door of the council chamber, and the Dauphin commanded that she should be admitted. Having entered, she fell on her knees before him, and said, "Noble Dauphin, do not hold such long councils; come to Rheims and receive your crown. I am commanded from above to lead you thither."

One of the bishops asked her how "the voices" made themselves intelligible to her, and the Dauphin pressed her to explain the matter. She replied that, being engaged in prayer and lamenting to God that her messages met with so much incredulity, she heard a voice saying, "Go on, my daughter, I will aid thee—go ;" and she said that when she heard that voice she was marvellously glad, and wished it would always speak. This discourse, delivered with the greatest simplicity, but with every sign of earnest piety, made a great impression on the assembly. Charles promised her that steps should be immediately taken to accomplish her desire, and an army was formed under the Duke of Alençon. It marched at first to Orleans, so lately the scene of her glory, and from thence proceeded to attack the Duke of Suffolk, who had entrenched himself at Jargeau, a town about ten miles distant from Orleans.

She summoned Suffolk to surrender in the usual style. "Surrender to the King of Heaven, and go your ways, or evil will happen to you." Suffolk wished for a truce ; this was refused, and the town was taken by assault. "The Maid," having set her foot on a ladder in order to mount to the rampart, an English soldier, with a large stone, struck her standard and hurled her into the trench. In an instant she was up again, cheering on her soldiers. Animated by her voice and daring, they rushed forward with an impetuosity which was utterly irresistible. The English gave way, and endeavoured to escape over the bridge into the castle, but they were hotly pursued, and Suffolk himself was taken prisoner, as was also his brother John.

From Jargeau the Maid advanced to Beaugency, the garrison of which was in no condition to resist. Meung followed the same example, and Talbot made a last stand at Patay. It is said that the English and French armies were separated by a forest, and the French knew not the exact locality of their enemy's camp. A stag bursting from a thicket before them rushed into the English lines, and the uproar which this incident created discovered their whereabouts. The French being thus almost miraculously guided, attacked their foes and utterly routed them. Talbot and others were taken prisoners; even the gallant Fastolfe fled; and about 2000 were slain.

Victory being secured, the tender nature of the Maid of Orleans could not be restrained. She pitied the vanquished; she descended from her horse to succour the wounded, comfort the dying, and with her own hands stanched and bound up the bleeding wounds of many.

Jeanne returned to the Dauphin, and again urged upon him the journey to Rheims. He still shrank from the difficulties with which such an expedition was beset, but his excuses had lost their former power, even if they did not assume the form of unbelief in "the daughter of God;" and at length the urgency of Jeanne, the enthusiasm of his troops, and the representation of his female favourites prevailed upon the vacillating prince, and the order was issued for the march upon Rheims.

VII.

THE MARCH TO RHEIMS AND CORONATION.

"The morn was fair
When Rheims re-echo'd to the busy hum
Of multitudes for high solemnity
Assembled."—SOUTHEY.

CHARLES set out from Gien at the head of a retinue numbering several thousands, which was largely ro-

inforced in the course of their progress. The fame of the
" Maid of Orleans" had spread considerably, and numbers flocked to her standard, though, perhaps, many from
motives of mere curiosity. They marched to Auxerre,
which was held by the Burgundians, and refused to open
its gates to the Dauphin, but supplied his army with
provisions for payment. From Auxerre they proceeded
in a north-easterly direction, and advanced upon Troyes,
which was also held by a strong Burgundian garrison.
It was not thought advisable to leave this important
town in a state of hostility, and Jeanne strongly advised
that it should be attacked. The chancellor of the Dauphin objected, that it would occupy too much time ;
whereupon Jeanne declared that it should be assaulted
and taken on the morrow. She commanded the trench
to be filled with faggots, stones, and whatever of that
nature could be obtained ; and the inhabitants, seeing
the determination of the besiegers, and believing, perhaps,
the invincibility of " The Maid," surrendered, the gates
were thrown open, and Charles entered the city as its
king.

It has been well observed that nothing succeeds like
success. Every victory achieved by " The Maid " was
the prelude and parent of victories yet to come. But
envy follows close upon the heels of popularity. Richard,
the monk, pretended to doubt her orthodox character,
and in the presence of the people, he actually presumed
to exorcise her as fearing that she was under Satanic
influence. Jeanne smiled, and said, " Do what you wish,
I shall not fly away."

From Troyes they proceeded northward to Chalons
sur Marne, which opened its gates enthusiastically to the
liberator of her country, and on the 16th July Charles
entered the ancient city of Rheims. He was attended

with a splendid retinue of noblemen and cavaliers, an immense concourse of citizens and peasants from the adjoining villages. Among others come to gaze upon this wondrous and exciting scene were Jeanne's father and her brothers, with feelings very different from those with which they had parted from her at Domremy. But Jeanne's feelings had known no change; she was still the tender, loving child and the affectionate sister. She received them with every mark of warm attachment, and her brothers, at her suggestion, attached themselves to the camp, and received distinguishing marks of the royal favour.

The next day, Sunday, the 17th July 1429, the coronation of Charles took place in the fine old cathedral of Rheims. The ceremony began at nine in the morning, and occupied nearly five hours. None of the usual formalities were omitted, and everything was done with the utmost preciseness and splendour. The king, in his robes of state, was conducted to his place in front of the altar, and repeated on his knees the words of the customary oath administered by the Archbishop of Rheims. He swore to keep and defend the faith, to do justice, to be merciful, and to maintain peace among his people; to suppress and banish all heretics. This done, two bishops raised him in his chair to show him to the people. Then came a flourish of trumpets, and the immense multitude shouted "Noel, Noel," the usual acclamation in France at the appearance of the king. The archbishop then anointed him with holy oil, which was supposed to render his person sacred. Then followed litanies, exhortations, and benedictions; and amid another flourish of trumpets and the shouts of "Noel, Noel," the crown of France was placed upon the head of Charles VII.

"The Maid of Orleans" had stood during this ceremony beside the altar bearing her beautiful banner, the
oriflamme of France.   It is impossible adequately to
describe the feelings which filled her heart at this accomplishment of her hopes, her prayers, and her labours.
Her heart overflowed with joy and with gratitude to
God, to whom she humbly ascribed all that had been
effected.   In the eyes of the people she was "the daughter
of God," a something supernatural, their prophetess, and
their champion.   Women held up their children to be
touched by her, as if she were an angel; soldiers bent
their knees to her standard, and thought it sanctified
their weapons to touch them with her naked sword.   But
she refused these marks of superstitious reverence, declaring that she was only the humble instrument of
God, and that all power proceeded from obedience to
His will.

The coronation rites were ended, and Charles was
sitting on his royal throne in all the pomp and dignity
of a king.   By his side stood the Maid, whose face
beamed with religious ardour and holy joy.   All eyes
were turned upon her, and a solemn silence pervaded the
assembly as, bending her standard, she came before the
king, and humbly kneeling, pronounced with tremulous
voice these words :

"O gentle king,* now is fulfilled the pleasure of God,
who ordained me to lead you to this city of Rheims to
receive your consecration.   Now you are truly king, and
the kingdom of France belongs to you."

* She had hitherto always addressed him as "Dauphin."

VIII.

THE COLLAPSE.

" My heart is wounded when I see such virtue
Afflicted by the weight of such misfortune."—ADDISON.

CHARLES could not be insensible of his deep obligations
to the Maiden from Lorraine, and he was not unwilling
to evince his gratitude. He conferred upon her the
rank of nobility, and permitted her to assume a coat of
arms, upon which was quartered the royal *fleur-de-lis*.
He promoted her brothers in the royal army, and ex-
empted her native village, Domremy, from taxation.
Jeanne might have had anything for the asking, and
this was her request:

" Permit me, gentle king, to return to my father and
mother, that I may live again the life that I used to lead
with them."

Jeanne must have felt in herself that her mission was
ended when she proffered this request, which her simplicity and sincerity of heart forbids to be regarded as
affectation.

Jeanne had entered into public life with the declaration that she was sent from God to raise the siege of
Orleans, and to crown the king at Rheims. These two
things had been effected, and her work was really accomplished. The ship of the state had been nearly
stranded, and she, with a mighty effort, had sent it into
deep water, where it was riding safely; it was not
necessary that she should follow it, and to do so was to
her own destruction. That yearning for home and peace
testified but too plainly that the Divine impulse which
had thus far urged her to combat and to war, had ceased.

She had descended from her sublime elevation, and her thoughts again touched earth.

But the king heard her modest request with astonishment not unequal in degree with which he had received her first communication. To lose her was to lose the visible *palladium* of the people, the idol of the army, the prop of the monarchy. It might be in all seriousness that she was not indispensable, for she was not skilled in military tactics, and was particularly averse to the shedding of blood; but the enthusiasm she inspired on the battle-field represented a force which could scarcely be measured.

The king entreated, remonstrated, and at last absolutely refused to sanction her departure. The army and the people prayed her to remain ever with them, their guide, champion, and deliverer. Jeanne hesitated, and complied, but not without sinister apprehension.

"I have only a year to remain with you," said she; "let us proceed."

The success and coronation of the king had brought corresponding depression into the allied camp of the Burgundians and the English. The Duke of Burgundy seemed unwilling to commit himself too deeply against the king, and the English were distracted by the jealousies existing between Bedford the regent and the Cardinal of Winchester. However the cardinal hastened with an army to the support of Bedford in Paris, as the siege of that city by Charles and his "miraculous Maid" appeared imminent.

Indeed after some manœuvring between the two hostile armies, the Duke of Bedford shut himself in the city, and prepared to sustain a siege. The French army appeared at St Denis, and Jeanne pressed the king to lose no time in giving the assault. She believed that the influence which had driven the English from Orleans, and opened the gates of Troyes and Rheims, would be no less effectual at Paris. But the English army had been largely reinforced; its hold upon the city was tenacious; its resolution to resist the contemplated attack was desperate; and even the citizens were too deeply compromised to anticipate with equanimity the restoration of Charles's authority, and permitted the base report to be spread that "the king and his witch had sworn to lay the city in ruins."

Jeanne well knew that an army can only acquire respect by an inflexible discipline. All violations of decency and morality excited in her a holy indignation. One day she was so far provoked as to strike an offender in this respect with the flat side of her sword—the sword which had been discovered by special revelation, and which had flashed at Orleans and Patay. It was broken by the blow. Such an occurrence, at any time discouraging, was in that age looked upon as undoubtedly of evil omen. Even the king was disturbed at it, and Jeanne herself could not refrain from tears. "But," said she, "I prefer my white standard and my little battle-axe. The sword never struck to kill, but to conquer, and an enemy's blood has never soiled it."

After a week of useless expectation, Jeanne led her troops to the assault. This was on the 8th September, a day appointed as a solemn festival by the Romish Church. Paris was scandalised at this seeming disregard of religious propriety, and the fact was remembered against her on her subsequent trial. She had promised that the king should sleep in his capital, and she advanced with an energy, and fought with a determination which seemed irresistible.

Notwithstanding a heavy fire from the city walls, she

led her troops across the first trench, but on arriving at
the second, it was found filled with water. While
seeking the shallowest part, and sounding for this purpose with her lance, she received an arrow from the
ramparts. Her standard-bearer was killed by her side,
and smarting with pain and weakened by loss of blood,
she fell fainting on a heap of the slain. She was carried
to the edge of the first trench, where she was in some
measure sheltered from the fire of the city, and stretched
upon the grass helpless, but not hopeless. She urged
renewed attack—declared that victory was to be had by
seeking it. In vain they begged her to retire from the
field—in vain they represented that the assault was
perfectly hopeless. She felt that death was preferable
to defeat, since defeat in this instance would be disgrace.
She struggled with fortune even against hope, and at
last the Duke of Alençon, fearing for her safety, and in
her for the spirit of the army, ordered his guard to carry
her in their arms from the field of carnage where she
wished to die.

This defeat, and the falsification of her confident prediction, had a most depressing effect upon the spirits of
the Maid. It was the first blow to her prestige, and
seemed to denote unmistakably that her judgment was
not only human but even unreliable. She began to
doubt whether, if she had ever a mission, it had not now
entirely and completely terminated. She humbled herself before God with crying and tears. She humbled
herself before the king, and asked his pardon for the
failure of the attack. She declared that henceforth she
would renounce the character of champion of France,
and accordingly she placed her beautiful white armour
and her sword upon the tomb of St Denis in fulfilment
of this vow. But the king and his generals knew too

well the practical value of the influence she exerted over
the minds of the army to permit this resolution to be
carried out. They remonstrated, they persuaded, they
supplicated, until her intended departure was made to
appear in her own sight like a heartless desertion of the
cause she had loved so warmly, for which she had fought
so well, and which, with this single exception, had pros-
pered so unexpectedly. Jeanne was a woman, and,
though her judgment pointed one way, her feelings
carried her in the opposite direction. She consented to
remain and be still their prophetess and champion,
although conscious in herself that she was no longer
under the special guidance of a heavenly inspiration.

Charles made the check before Paris an excuse for
retiring into winter quarters, and he betook himself to
Chinon, where he was soon immersed in the frivolities
that had such attractions for that weak and irresolute
monarch. The celebrated French historian, Sismondi,*
says—"The unwarlike citizens of Champagne, Picardy,
and the Isle of France were now rising or conspiring to
throw off the English yoke, knowing well that if they
failed no mercy would be shown to them, and that they
would perish by the hangman's hand. Yet they boldly
exposed themselves in order to replace their king on his
throne, and this king, far from imitating their generosity,
could not even bear the hardships of a camp or the toils
of business for more than two months and a half; he
would not any longer consent to forego his festivals, his
dances, or his other less innocent delights."

Jeanne spent the winter chiefly at Bourges. Of her
private life during this interval we have little or no
record, but it is not difficult to understand that the
atmosphere and occupations of the Court were out of

* Died 1842.

unison with the ideas and feelings of the peasant maid. She was probably greatly occupied in improving the discipline of the army, of whom she was at once the patron and the pride.

With the return of spring came the renewal of hostilities. On the battle-field Jeanne seemed to recover her spirits and her inspiration. Her energy in rallying the retreating ranks, her audacity in heading the charge or leading to the assault were undiminished, and after some signal successes she resolved to march to the relief of Compiègne, then besieged by the Duke of Burgundy. The commander of the city was Flavy, a bold but unprincipled man, who is believed to have been influenced by a bribe from the Duke of Burgundy, and to have been jealous of the honour accorded to the Maid. Jeanne declared that the town should be saved, but it was observed that she seemed depressed, and she expressed herself in fear of treachery. "I do not think I shall be with you at the Feast of St John" were the words in which she gave utterance to her feelings of foreboding.

Having entered Compiègne (May 24) she immediately headed a sortie of the garrison against the besiegers with her usual audacity and impetuosity. Mounted on her noble charger, she carried her standard in her hand, and over her armour she had a mantle of cloth of gold. Twice repulsed, she rallied her troops, and again led them to the charge. At last the allied forces of the Burgundians and the English concentrated their efforts upon the band which fought around the Maid as her body-guard, and who, becoming outnumbered and pressed by the foe, urged her to regain the city. But Jeanne, who had never exhibited greater valour and self-possession, declared that victory would not desert her standard if they were only true to themselves, and attacked the enemy with determination. Finding at last that her men were being overpowered, she gave the signal for retreat, but, maintaining the post of honour and of danger, she followed last on the rear-guard. Her troops had crossed the drawbridge safely, and she herself had just spurred her horse to cross also when the drawbridge was suddenly raised. Isolated and undefended, she was speedily surrounded by her foes. She fought desperately, and had her own people made an effort to save her, it is more than probable she might have escaped. It is said that an archer seized her by her mantle and pulled her off her horse. She rose to her feet instantly, and fought with such fury that she made those before her recoil with astonishment and fear. At last, overwhelmed by increasing numbers, and seeing all hope of deliverance gone, she surrendered herself to the bastard of Vendôme, and was conducted to Lionel of Ligny, the general of the Duke of Burgundy.

No victory could have equalled in the estimation of the allied troops this trophy, which either accident or treachery had placed in their hands. To them the Maiden from Lorraine was the personification of France. In holding her they seemed to hold the fortunes of the kingdom. From all parts of the camp they poured out to assure themselves of the fact, and the air was filled with shouts of triumph. The Duke of Burgundy could scarcely credit the report, and hastened to assure himself of its accuracy. He was overjoyed at the event, and immediately issued a proclamation to his own subjects, in which he informed them of this surprising capture, which he ascribed to " the pleasure of our blessed Creator."

IX.

IMPRISONMENT.

"Tread thou the path that leads thee to the grave,
Rough though it be, and painful."

CAPTURED, but not conquered, the indomitable spirit of
the heroic Maiden struggled against duress as a newly-
taken bird against the bars of its prison. She had lived
only for her king and her country, and could not understand how their interests could be advanced by her withdrawal from the scene. According to the laws of chivalry,
she was entitled to respectful and hospitable treatment,
and to be exchanged upon demand for a prisoner of
equal rank, or else to be liberated for ransom. But conflicting interests were at work, of which Jeanne was to
be the victim. Lionel of Ligny, to whom she had surrendered, was the vassal of the Lord of Luxembourg,
and anxious to secure his favour, made over to him the
invaluable prisoner. The Lord of Luxembourg, less
bitter towards the unfortunate Maiden than her fellow-
countrymen, transferred her to his castle of Beaurevoir,
where she was honourably and kindly treated by the ladies
of the family. They urged her to assume female attire,
and this she consented to do, fully explaining to them her
reasons for having hitherto done otherwise, and which
they could comprehend and sympathise with. Here she
remained, but her heart was with the people; and her
only anxiety was lest the cause for which she had fought
so well should suffer in her absence. Sensible that she
had done nothing to incur the displeasure of Heaven, she
seems to have persuaded herself that her impatience
would be forgiven, and that even a miraculous interposi-

tion would be granted.   She had yet to learn that "They
also serve who only stand and wait."   Believing that the
arm which had strengthened her at Orleans, reanimated her
at Jargeau, and shielded her at Paris, would not be with-
drawn from her trusting reliance, she precipitated herself from the summit of the tower to fly to the relief of
Compiègne. She fell to the ground stunned, and was
taken up apparently lifeless. By the assiduous attentions of her female friends she was restored, but though
no limbs were fractured, her hopes and spirits were
utterly broken, and she only asked to be allowed to
die.

This circumstance concurring with the self interest of
the court of Luxembourg, led to her removal from
Beaurevoir. She was delivered into the power of the
Duke of Burgundy, and by his order conveyed to Arras,
a fortified town on the river Scarpe. Importunate requests
were made under English influence to treat her otherwise
than as a prisoner of war. Her bitterest enemy seems
to have been the Bishop of Beauvais, who left not a
stone unturned to bring her to trial as a witch. This
he did not from any pious horror of witchcraft, but from
motives of the most unworthy and sordid character.

Normandy and Paris were at this time under the do-
minion of the English, and the Archbishopric of Rouen,
then, as now, a wealthy and important city, was vacant.
Cauchon, the Bishop of Beauvais, had set his heart upon
this rich piece of preferment, and thought if he could
gratify the English by the acquisition of the Maid of
Orleans, they would requite him by using their influence
in obtaining his elevation to the see of Rouen. Cardinal
Winchester was then *de facto* regent of England; his
influence at Rome was immense; there was no reason to
doubt that his nominee would be received with all con-

sideration at the Vatican. To secure his friendship, therefore, was the great anxiety of the Bishop of Beauvais; and as the cardinal was a believer in sorcery—a crime which he himself had imputed to Gloucester, the king's uncle—it was supposed that it would be a gratification to him if Jeanne could be brought to trial upon a charge of witchcraft. Cauchon therefore wrote to the University of Paris, then under English influence, and succeeded in obtaining their authority for such a trial. The Vicar-general of the Inquisition wrote thus to the Duke of Burgundy :

" We require and earnestly enjoin, in the name of the faith and under the penalties of justice, that you send and bring prisoner before us Jeanne, suspected of crimes, to be proceeded against by the Holy Inquisition."

But the request of the bishop and the university decree might have been disregarded had not Cauchon been enabled to offer more potent solicitations. To secure the person of the Maid, the English were ready to offer almost any price. The bishop, who seems to have sold his very soul to the enemies of his country, was authorised by them to write thus to the Dukes of Burgundy and Luxembourg :

"Although that woman ought not to be considered as a prisoner of war, nevertheless, to recompense those who have taken and retained her, the king (of England) will give to them 6000 francs, and to the bastard of Vendôme, who captured her, an annuity of £300."

A further consideration was pressed upon the Duke of Burgundy. The woollen trade of Flanders, a source of very considerable yearly profit, was then mainly in the hands of the English, and an intimation that this trade might be diverted, or perhaps annihilated, was a hint not to be disregarded.

During these negotiations, Jeanne was removed from Arras to Le Crohy, from whence she could see the English camp. No doubt now remained in her mind as to her impending fate, and in the month of November 1430, she was formally delivered into the hands of those who were thirsting for her blood.

The inquiry naturally arises here, Where was Charles VII.? Had he done nothing for the rescue or the ransom of one to whom he owed so much, and if not, why not? It is difficult to avoid imputing to that monarch either base ingratitude or cruel indifference, but he is not the only instance which History has afforded to illustrate the sacred warning—" Put not your trust in princes." Charles had readily used the Maid to advance his own interests, but he was not the person to engage in any troublesome negotiation or expedition that might by possibility be avoided. His lethargic spirit could not easily be aroused to exertion, and it quailed in the presence of difficulty. Jeanne was left to her fate mainly because her sovereign had not energy sufficient to endeavour to avert it. As to the obligations, it is enough to say that the ingratitude of kings is proverbial. An attempt, indeed, has been made to clear the character of the king by laying the blame upon his chancellor, as in after-days our own Elizabeth sought to transfer to her secretary the odium and the guilt of the death of the Scottish queen. The French chancellor, it is said, had orders to negotiate for the liberation of the captive Maid, but that instigated by an unworthy jealousy he failed, that is to say, he neglected to bring the negotiation to a successful termination. It would not be unreasonable to assume that the English, animated by a spirit of vindictiveness against her who had been to them the cause of so many disasters, would have refused every offer for her deliverance, but, to the deep dishonour of her own countrymen, there is no substantial record that efforts were seriously made in behalf of their champion.

X.

NEED OF WITNESSES.

" They sought false witness—but found none."

AMID the savage exultation of her foes, and the silent commisseration of those who dared not to make any overt demonstration, Jeanne was conducted a prisoner into Rouen, the residence at that period of the young English king (Henry VI.) and his principal officers. She was led, guarded and in fetters, through the thronged streets of the city, and secured in the tower of the old chateau. A sinister foreboding of her doom found vent in the half-hysterical exclamation, "Why is all this!" She had resumed her manly attire upon leaving Beaurevoir, and found in it a protection from the brutal insults to which she was exposed from a licentious soldiery. Her youth, valour, and misfortune, far from exciting a chivalrous composure on the part of her gaolers, seemed only to incite the worst instincts of their nature. Nothing was spared that could aggravate her distress, nothing left untried to accomplish her ruin. Sentinels watched her room night and day, and she had reason to fear the worst outrages from those appointed to guard her. The Bishop of Beauvais urged on the trial. A priest calling himself Lorrain, and who pretended to be a fellow-countryman of the Maid, was imprisoned with

her under the pretence of being a favourer of Charles
VII. He insinuated himself into the confidence of
Jeanne, in whose heart compassion for others was not
extinguished by her own misfortunes. An apparent
interchange of mutual sympathies was in effect only a
treacherous method of obtaining secrets; and even the
priestly office was prostituted to the same purpose.
Acting as her confessor, this Lorrain became possessed
of facts and feelings which otherwise would have been
confined to the breast of the prisoner. The bishop even
condescended to play the eaves-dropper on those solemn
occasions, and indeed no artifice seems to have been left
untried to condemn the unfortunate Maiden out of her
own mouth. And yet, such is the strength of truth
and honesty, all these attempts proved useless. The
brightest silver may be for a moment tarnished by a
breath, but soon throws off the taint, and resumes its
wonted lustre. Disloyalty of any kind, whether to her God,
her king, or herself, had no place in the heart of Jeanne.
God, in whom she had trusted, and whose Divine messen-
gers she believed had guided her, might seem to have
forsaken her; the prince for whom she had fought so
well might seem to have forgotten her; the Church of
her baptism, whose services she had so highly prized,
might seem to have turned against her; all human
sympathy might seem shut up from her, and yet she
sinned not with her lips. Her enemies found that
nothing which was drawn from her could be turned to
her condemnation.

Whatever depression Jeanne might have felt, her faith
and fortitude did not fail to assert themselves when
occasion required. The Count of Luxembourg, whose
prisoner she had been, and who had so basely sold her to
the enemy, being at Rouen, expressed a desire to see his

former captive, and was accordingly conducted to her
prison by the Earls of Strafford and Warwick.   Will it
be believed that these three noblemen could find pleasure
in trifling with the feelings and witnessing the suffering
of one who had been the champion of one nation and the
terror of the other?

"Jeanne," said Luxembourg ironically, "I am come
to ransom you, on condition that you promise not to arm
against us any more."

"Ah," replied the poor prisoner, with an accent of
reproach, "you are laughing at me. You have neither
the power nor the will.   I well know that the English
will kill me, hoping to gain the kingdom by my death;
but were they a hundred thousand more than they are,
they should not have this kingdom."

Strafford drew his dagger, and the dauntless Maiden
would have sealed her brave defiance with her blood but
for the intervention of the Earl of Warwick, who restrained the furious Strafford, and postponed a murder
which was yet to be accomplished.

Meanwhile, the preparations for her so-called trial
were carried forward.   But, as in the greatest judicial
investigation in History, it was necessary to obtain false
witnesses, in order to accomplish the object in view, so
the enemies of the Maid were in some difficulty to procure such evidence as would incriminate her.   Emis-
saries had been despatched to Domremy to rake up
village scandal, and to seek for crimes in her very
infancy.   But they had lost their labour.   The memory
of the just is blessed, and it is no small testimony to the
character of Jeanne that her native village testified unreservedly and unanimously to the earnestness of her
devotion and the purity of her life.   The companions of
her early youth spake with tears of her gentleness and

truth, her compassion for others, and her deep devotion.
The villagers all had a good word for Jeanne, and the
would-be informers retired disconcerted, feeling that they
had nothing to hope for in Domremy.

Equally unfortunate were they elsewhere.   Like vul-
tures allured by tainted atmosphere, they turned their
attention to whatever place seemed to savour of a
calumny.   But still no false witnesses could be found ;
the soldiers spoke of the Maid with enthusiasm, the
people with gratitude, which was evinced not unfre-
quently by aspirations for her deliverance.   It was
necessary to use the basest of instruments to procure
even the semblance of a charge against her, and accordingly, as already alluded to, perfidy of the worst type
was employed to effect what truth and justice would
have failed to accomplish.

XI.

THE TRIAL.

" The purest treasure mortal times afford
Is—spotless reputation"—SHAKESPEARE.

ON the 9th January 1431, commenced at Rouen one of
those solemn farces—a trial with a foregone conclusion.
The Bishop of Beauvais sat on the judgment-seat, and
beside him the Vicar of the Inquisition.   Lawyers and
divines were gathered together to the number of nearly
one hundred, in order to debate the great question
whether or not the peasant girl who had led to victory
the armies of France, was an instrument in the hands of
Satan.   The bishop submitted for the consideration of

this assembly such evidence as had already been collected, but it was found to be so unsatisfactory and unreliable that the charge of witchcraft could not be sustained. Here then was a chance of escape. The accused had been indicted for a certain crime, the indictment had failed. Justice would have set the prisoner free, but justice was not the purpose or the object of this infamous trial. Whatever happened, Jeanne was not to be allowed to escape death. She was not a witch, but perhaps she was a *heretic!*

In those days, now happily gone by for ever, when the Church of Rome was in full possession of all the powers of government, when she could seize with the spiritual arm and destroy with the temporal, not the least terrible of her resources was the charge of heresy. Men trembled and turned pale at the accusation, and, in most cases, when it was formally charged, nothing was to be hoped for,—it only remained to prepare to die.

On 21st February, everything being ready for the trial, Jeanne appeared before her judges. Her sweet and modest countenance had lost none of its firmness of expression, though showing marks of anxiety and sorrow. Attired in her warrior dress she stood, the impersonation of her country, in the power of her foes. The sight of a tender and defenceless maiden—who had united the courage of a warrior and the tenderness of a woman; who had gained battles, captured cities, crowned a monarch, and saved a kingdom, now brought to trial for her life, for some supposed unsoundness in her faith—might have touched hearts more stern even than we should expect to find in a Christian bishop and doctors of theology.

Jeanne was exhorted by the president of the council * to speak the truth in all that should be demanded of her.

---

* The Bishop of Beauvais.

She replied that she did not know what those things might be; that they might be such as she could not speak about, but she ultimately promised solemnly to answer unreservedly in all that appertained to her faith. She declared, in answer to inquiries, that she was nineteen years of age; that in her native place she was called Jehannette, and in France, Jehanne. She complained of the fetters on her limbs. The bishop reminded her that she had attempted several times before to escape, and that she was chained for security. She replied: "It is true I have attempted to do so; nor is it unlawful. No one can say I have broken my promise, for I never promised."

She was ordered to repeat the Lord's Prayer and the Ave Maria, and it has been suggested that this was from a superstitious idea that if she was really possessed by the devil, she could not be able to pronounce such holy words. But surely it might have occurred to learned theological doctors that the prince of darkness is able to transform himself into an angel of light, and that the mere mechanical utterance of pious phrases would be no insuperable bar to such a master of devices, who has, moreover, shown his ability to quote Scripture even in the most exalted presence. Jeanne, however, replied that she would willingly repeat them if the bishop would hear her confession.

This appeal, so full of confidence and conscious innocence, in which she offered to make of even her judge and her enemy a spiritual father and the depositary of secrets, to be whispered to none other, was too irregular to be conceded, but too touching to be disregarded. For once the heart of the bishop was moved, and he suspended the sitting for the rest of the day.

At her next appearance she seemed less diffident in

answering. She confessed to having heard heavenly
voices; but pressed to declare what those voices had said
to her, she hesitated. "I cannot say all that they told
me," she replied, "and I have greater fear of displeasing
them, than in replying to you. I beg you not to require
it of me."

The bishop asked her if speaking the truth was a sin,
and she replied: "My voices have told me certain things
not for you, but for the king;" and she added with sublime enthusiasm: "I am come from God, and have nothing to do here. Send me back to God from whom I
have come. You say you are my judge; have a care
what you are doing, for truly I am sent by God, and you
are putting yourself in great danger."

This simple and touching declaration was met by one
of those subtle and perfidious questions which only a
captious theologian could put: "Jeanne, do you believe
you are in a state of grace?"

The reply, whether affirmative or negative, was equally
difficult and equally dangerous;* but with that admirable tact which is so characteristic of woman, she met
the difficulty thus:

"If I am not, I pray God to put me in it; if I am, I
pray God to preserve me therein."

Well says the historian, "the Pharisees were stu-
pefied."

But the question, like a barbed arrow, rankled and
fretted. After that sublime reply, she returned: "Oh,
if I were sure that I was not in a state of grace, I should
be the most wretched person in the world. But if I had
been in sin, surely 'the voice' would not have spoken to

* It is recorded that one of the assessors could not forbear the remark, that
the question was so difficult that the prisoner was not bound to answer it; but
he was quickly silenced by the unscrupulous bishop.

me. I only wish that each of you could have heard it also."

This language, so far from softening her judges, only seemed to have redoubled their hate and malignity. Questions of all sorts and upon all subjects were forced upon her, with the only apparent object of destroying her. Had the voices told her to hate the Burgundians? Did she not, as a girl, visit the fairy tree? Did she fast on the days of abstinence? Was she certain that she had seen St Catherine and St Michael? One question alone is sufficient to show the mental and moral condition of her judges: "Was St Michael naked?" To this infamous interrogation she replied with all the simplicity of celestial purity: "Do you think, then, that our Lord has not wherewith to clothe him?"

Other whimsical questions followed. Had St Michael a body? Had he limbs? Were the figures that appeared in the likeness of angels? On this subject every possible form of question was put to catch her tripping, yet she answered without reserve, and with all the confidence of well-founded faith.

From this mysterious subject they passed to the military question.

"Did not the soldiers make standards in imitation of yours?"

"Did you not say that those standards would be lucky?"

To this last she replied: "No, I only said, go in boldly among the English, and I will follow you."

"But why was your standard carried in the church at Rheims at the coronation, rather than those of the other captains?"

Answer—"It had had the peril; it was only right it should have the honour."

" What was the motive of the people who kissed your hands, feet, and clothing ?"

" The poor folk willingly honoured me because I treated them kindly, I sustained and defended them to the utmost of my power. Their wives and daughters touched their rings with mine, but I did not perceive in that any bad intentions. Whilst I was at Rheims, at Chateau Thierry, at Lagny, it is true that many requested me to be god-mother to their children, and I consented."

Interrogations of this character, and such simple common-sense replies could scarcely fail to have some effect even upon her judges. Indeed, an impression favourable to the prisoner was becoming evident, and the bishop thought it better to proceed with new assessors and a smaller number of judges. The place of examination was changed from the castle of Rouen to the prison, and it was resolved to proceed with closed doors. The bishop was now less scrupulous, because he had received the assurance of the support of the Inquisition.*

To the inquiry did the voices impel her to the sortie at Compiègne, she replied, somewhat indirectly—" They told me I should be taken before Monseigneur; that it was necessary for me that I must not be astonished at it, but take it in good part, and that God would aid me ; " and then she added, after a pause—" Since it has pleased God it should be so, it is all for the best."

" Do you think you did well to leave home without the permission of your father and mother ? Must we not honour our parents ?"

Answer—"They have pardoned me."

" Do you not think you were sinning in acting thus ?"

Answer—" God commanded it. Although I had had a hundred fathers and mothers I should have gone."

* 12th March.

" What have the voices called you ? "

Answer—" Before the siege of Orleans was raised, and since, the voices have called me ' Jehanne la Pucelle, daughter of God.' "

" Was it well to attack Paris on the fête de Notre Dame ? " She replied—" It is quite right to observe the fêtes of Notre Dame, and holy to observe them always."

Another insidious question, implying that she had an idea of suicide was put.   " Why did you leap from the tower of Beaurevoir ? "

Answer—" I heard that the poor folks of Compiègne would all be killed, even the children, and I knew also that I myself was sold to the English, and I would rather die than be in the hands of the English."

" Was it right to try to escape when you had been informed you were to be taken ? "

Answer—" I would fly now if God permitted it."

" Will you give us the sign which you gave to the Dauphin to show him that you came on the part of God ? "

" I have told you already that what concerns the Dauphin I will never declare.   Go and ask him."

" Did you not demand male attire from the queen when you were presented to her ? "

" It is true."

" Have you not been invited to lay aside your warlike costume and to resume woman's dress ? "

" Yes, certainly ; and I have always replied that I would change my dress only by the command of God." She admitted also that the daughter of the Count of Luxembourg and the lady of Beaurevoir had begged her, when a prisoner under their care, to forego the male attire, and that if she could have conscientiously done so, she would willingly have pleased them in such a matter, so

strong was the impression that their kindness had made
upon her.

Being asked if prayers had not been offered in her
name both in the camp and in the towns, she replied—
" If the people have prayed in my name I am ignorant
of it. They have not done so with my approval. If they
have prayed for me I do not think there is much harm
in that. But I never pretended to do miracles."

She was asked if there was any magic in the ring
which she wore on her finger, and why she so often
looked upon that ring in the field of battle, and she
answered it was because the name of Jesus was engraved
upon it, and because it recalled to her the pleasures of
home.

Attacked on all points with questions of the most
abstruse and subtle nature, her character had emerged
uninjured. Her native simplicity and integrity had
been, as it were, a breastplate of steel, from which the
darts of her enemies fell pointless. It only remained to
try the force of some questions of conscience.

She was asked if she would submit everything to the
authority of the Church ?

Jeanne hesitated.

The term church has different meanings, and it is
doubtful if she fully realised the signification in which
the word was used on this occasion. The first idea in
her mind would be the well-known and well-loved church
of her native village, the kind and fatherly curé, whose
presence and words were always welcome. To this
authority she would unhesitatingly submit. But there
was another aspect under which the Church was presented to her mind, viz., the Bishop of Beauvais, and
with all due deference to his office, she had no reason to
regard him favourably. The question being repeated,

she replied, and would give no other response—"I must refer everything to the King of Heaven, who has sent me."

They reminded her that the Church was twofold. That there was (1.) The Church triumphant, consisting of God, the saints, and the spirits made perfect; and (2.) The Church militant, represented by the pope, his cardinals, the clergy, and all good Christians, that this part of the Church in council assembled cannot err, but is guided and governed by the Holy Spirit. And she was asked if she would not submit to this Church militant.

"I am come," said she, "to the King of France on the part of God, of the Virgin Mary, the saints of the Church triumphant. To that Church I submit myself and all my acts done or to be done."

"And what as to the Church militant?"

She replied, "I have nothing further to say."

The sublime simplicity of these replies gave a turn to the trial very dangerous for the accused. It was really an appeal from the earthly tribunal to the heavenly one, and had a tendency to subvert all human courts of justice. Concession to such an appeal would be a confession on the part of society of inability to deal with crime. And yet there have been occasions when such an attitude has been felt to be fully justified by the circumstances under which the prisoner has been placed, and by the ill-concealed corruption and tyranny of the judges.

There were, however, present at the trial three persons who heard the simple and touching answers of the Maid, and heard them with some degree of emotion. Though in no way disposed to favour her pretensions, they felt they could not conscientiously see her condemned without affording her every chance to which she was legally entitled. It was true that she had appealed exclusively to "the King of Heaven," but the pope was then be-

lieved to be Christ's vicar on earth, the centre and
fountain of all authority in this world, human and
divine, and they did not doubt that if Jeanne clearly
understood this, she would readily submit, and, by
appealing to Rome, obtain at least the benefit of an im-
partial trial. They accordingly boldly visited her in
prison, explained the matter fully to her, assured her
that an appeal to the pope was her undoubted privilege
and right, and urged her to avail herself of it. Following this advice, Jeanne next day solemnly appealed to
the pope in council, and thus virtually took the proceedings out of the hands of Cauchon and his assessors. One
is strongly here reminded of the celebrated appeal of
Paul to Cæsar, by which he saved himself from crafty
adversaries and an unjust judge. But the Christian
bishop was less scrupulous than the Roman pro-consul.
He was furious at the sight of his prey escaping; he demanded to know how she had obtained information of
this procedure, and such was the pressure brought to
bear upon Jeanne's advisers in this matter that they
thought it prudent to disappear, and with them was removed the last hope of Jeanne's deliverance.

Perhaps there is no greater testimony to the infamy
of this so-called trial than the opinion of its early proceedings, delivered by Jehan Lohier, one of the most
celebrated legists of Rouen. He declared that "the
trial was informal, that the assessors were not free, that
it was held with closed doors, and that the accused, a
simple peasant girl, was not capable of answering upon
such profound matters, and before such learned doctors;"
and also, "that the process involved the honour of the
prince, whose cause the Maid had espoused; that it was
necessary to summon him also, and cause him to appear
before the tribunal."

Even the theologians were far from unanimous in their opinions of the Maid and her pretensions, in spite of the garbled extracts from her answers which had been submitted to them. The charges against her resolved themselves into an enthusiastic belief that she had conversed with saints and angels, and to deny the possibility of this would have been to deny the marvellous legends of the "Lives of the Saints." It is therefore not surprising to find the venerable Bishop of Avranches replying "that after the doctrines of St Thomas, there was nothing impossible in what the Maiden asserted, and nothing that should be lightly rejected;" or to hear the Bishop of Lisieux declare "that her revelations might have been demoniacal, if they were not delusions, and that she needed only to submit herself to the Church."

"It was a strange sight," says Michelet, "to see these theologians, these learned doctors, labouring with all their force to overturn the foundation of their doctrine and the religious principle of the Middle Ages, a belief in revelation, a faith in the intervention of supernatural beings. They doubted at least those of angels, but their faith in the devil was entire." *

XII.

THE CONDEMNATION.

"This, damsel, is thy fate."—SOUTHEY.

WITH whatever degree of the supernatural fancy and romance may have invested Jeanne Darc, her inconsis-

* Histoire de France, tome v. 139.

tencies and weaknesses demonstrated clearly that she
was "only a woman." Thus, in the matter of appeal to
the pope, she sometimes offered entire submission, and
asked to be sent to him. Anon she reserved submission
only in matters of faith, and refused it as regarded all
she had *done*, and at other times appealed solemnly and
unreservedly and exclusively "to her King, the Judge
of heaven and earth."

Who does not see in all this the signs of that internal
conflict wherein the soul struggles for supremacy? The
alternations of hope and fear, the resolves and the re-
resolves, the shadows cast by the fear of man, the weakness arising from self-distrust, the intense longing for
more light, and at last the noble resolution to stand
upon some principle or to maintain some truth, even if it
involve the loss of all things—such are the experiences
of spirits truly heroic.

But the spirit is often willing while the flesh is weak.
Indeed, the agitation of the soul is the shattering of the
body, as the struggles of the embryo burst the case of
the chrysalis. Jeanne fell sick. Her malady commenced on Palm Sunday 1431, and yet on the following
Tuesday she was constrained to appear before her judges.
She was then informed that "they desired to proceed
gently and without demanding vengeance or corporal
punishment," that they wished to enlighten her in the
way of truth and salvation. She replied, "I thank you
very much for the admonitions which you give me, but
I have no intention of departing from the counsel of our
Lord."

Being asked if she would submit to the Church, she
replied, "I shall submit only to the Church of Heaven,
to God, the Virgin, and the Saints in Paradise. I have
never failed in Christian faith, and I desire not to do so."

The great point on which her judges appeared to be scandalised was her persistence in wearing manly attire. Whatever utility it may have had on the battle-field, it seemed to be mere bravado to wear it in prison after admonition. According to the Canon law it is an abominable thing in the sight of God for a woman to assume the dress of a man, overlooking the fact that Adam and Eve must have been identical in their fig leaf costume and their coats of skins; that the early progenitors of the human race could have indulged in no very great variety of dress, and that to this day in the tropics and at the poles it would be difficult to distinguish by their habiliments man from woman. The great legists of the Mediæval Church have stigmatised as a sin, only to be purged by penance, the assumption of male attire by a female. Jeanne was asked if she would disuse it. She hesitated, and asked time to consider. Being pressed to give it up, she replied she could not promise. Being threatened with deprivation of the consolations of religious worship, she nevertheless refused compliance. At last she hesitated, and begged to be allowed to join in worship, and that she might be supplied with a *very long* dress.

With true maiden modesty she did not, she could not explain to a large assembly of men her true reason for retaining her warrior dress. "It is necessary to know," says Michelet, "that three soldiers slept in her chamber; that, secured to a post by an iron chain, she was almost at their mercy; the manly dress which she wore was her only safeguard." It is difficult to repress one's indignation at the too evident design sanctioned or connived at by those in authority.

Watched from without, insulted by those within, tortured in body, wearied in mind, deprived of the con-

solations of religion, forsaken of all by the Church she
had loved so well, by the saints who had formerly sustained her, and apparently by God himself — what
wonder that she fell sick, became delirious and smitten
with fever !

Suspicion has been expressed that she was poisoned.
The Bishop of Beauvais, it is said, wished thus to get rid
of a troublesome matter.   But the Earl of Warwick had
quite other ideas, and on learning the nature of her condition, he said, " she must be cured by all means ; let her
not die a natural death.   The king has bought her, and
that at a great price, and she must die by the hands of
justice."   He would more truly have said by the hands
of cruelty and injustice.

Means were used for her recovery, which nevertheless
for some days appeared doubtful.   Her judges visited
her in prison.   Submission to the Church was the point
on which was to turn the salvation of her soul.   The
poor invalid, trembling with weakness, exclaimed—" Let
God do His pleasure with me.   I should like to confess,
to receive my Saviour, and to be buried in holy ground."
" But if you wish to have the sacraments of the Church
it is necessary to submit to the Church."   She made no
reply, and the judge repeating his words, she answered—
" If my body dies in prison, I hope you will bury it in
holy ground ; if you do not, I shall report the matter to
our Lord."

The judges were incessant in their endeavours to wring
from her an admission of subjection to the Church, and
at last one of them exclaimed—" If you do not obey the
Church you will be abandoned as an infidel."   She
replied—" I am a good Christian ; I have been baptized ;
I shall die as a good Christian."

After this Jeanne recovered her health, and to a great

degree her firmness of spirit. The agony of the Holy
Week, though not relieved by the Easter festivities (in
which she was not allowed to share), had been mollified
by meditations on the sufferings of Christ, of which His
people must in some shape or other be partakers. Her
answers were more grave, more firm ; and her appeal to
God was to Him alone, and not as before " to God and
the pope." The bitterness of death had passed, the
cost of the great sacrifice she was called upon to make
had been fully counted, the fear of man had subsided,
and the noble soul of the devoted Maiden seemed already
to be pluming its wings for a flight. When on the 11th
May they brought the executioner into her chamber,
declaring she was about to be put to the torture, she was
able to reply, with a courage which astonished her
judges, and actually assisted the sympathies of one in her
favour—" If you tear my limbs asunder and my soul from
my body I shall say nothing but what I have said."

The progress of the trial carried on by the bishop and
his assessors was not sufficiently rapid to satisfy the
Earl of Warwick or the Cardinal Winchester. The
latter therefore resolved to submit the matter to the judgment of the University of Paris. The reputation of the
Sorbonne then and for centuries afterwards stood high,[*]
and its decisions were received with little less reverence
than those of the pope himself. But Paris at this time
was held by English troops, and dominated by English
influence. It had resisted the appeal and the attack of
the Maid at the head of her troops, it had been shocked
by her permitting the assault to be made on a Church
festival, and while neither advocate or evidence were
heard in her favour, the articles of impeachment sub-

* Our own Henry VIII. submitted the question of the legality of his marriage with Catherine to the judgment of this University.

mitted to the consideration of the University were drawn
up by no friendly hand. It is therefore not surprising
that, without any delay, the Sorbonne formally and
solemnly decided (1.) That she was a child of the devil;
(2.) That she had been impious towards her parents;
(3.) That the Christian blood in her was tainted. It
may startle us that a judgment so overwhelming could
have been founded upon premises so limited and one-
sided; but what will men not say of that which is seen
through their prejudices? Was it not said of the finest
character recorded in history—" If he were not a male-
factor we would not have delivered him up !"

It was now resolved to try the effect of a public degradation. The popular sentiment was turning in her
favour, and it was thought desirable to divert the current. Accordingly, on the 23d May, a great public
spectacle was prepared. In the cemetery of St Ouen,
behind the noble church which now bears that name,
two large platforms were erected. One was occupied by
the Cardinal Winchester, representing the royal authority of England; by the Bishop of Beauvais, representing
"ambitious servility selling its country for honours," *
with judges, clergy, lawyers, and assessors. Upon the
opposite platform appeared " the delegated Maiden," in
her warrior dress, but in fetters, guarded by hussars.
Notaries were in attendance to take down her words, for
it was hoped that from weakness or fear some admission
might be drawn from her and turned against her. The
executioner, on his car, was in attendance, ready to
carry her off as soon as condemnation should be pronounced. The place was filled by an immense crowd
divided in opinion between respect for constituted
authority, superstitious fear of a witch, and pity for the

* Lamartine.

young and beautiful girl, whose only crime was that she had saved her country. A sermon was delivered by a celebrated preacher, whose eloquent zeal must have out-run his judgment when he exclaimed—"O noble house of France, thou who hast always been a defender of the faith, how couldst thou be so perverted as to attach thy-self to heresy and schism;" and when, pointing with his finger, he went on to say—"Yes, Jeanne, I tell thee thy king is a heretic and a schismatic!"

Crushed and broken as was the spirit of the Maid, an attack upon the character of her Dauphin was not for a moment to be borne. All thought of self was forgotten; a noble resentment illumined every feature of her pale and care-worn face as she exclaimed, interrupt-ing the preacher: "By my faith, I swear that he is the most noble Christian of all, and that he loves the Church, and is nothing of that which you say!"

The bishop imposed silence upon her, and the preacher concluded, doubtless feeling that he had not been en-tirely successful.

Then followed the usual unmeaning inquiry whether she had anything to say why condemnation should not be pronounced, it being perfectly understood that what-ever she might say would be treated as idle words. Jeanne must have felt the hopelessness of her situation. The animus of her judges, the protracted trial, the brutal confinement, the studied degradation, the malice of the English in whose power she knew herself to be, the desertion by her own countrymen, and, what was still more overwhelming, her apparent desertion by the Divine powers, under whose commission she had acted in these considerations, was the bitterness of death. An ordinary spirit would have been utterly crushed under misfortunes so unmitigated.

The Maiden rose; every eye was directed towards her,
every ear was strained to catch the sound of her voice.
Recalling to mind what she had been informed as to her
undoubted privilege as a prisoner, she exclaimed in a
clear, unfaltering, but not defiant voice, "I appeal to
the pope;" thus asserting at once her unquestionable
right, and also her membership of the Catholic Church.

The appeal was of course rejected. She had been
tried, it was averred, and found guilty of heresy and
witchcraft, and to these two deadly sins was added the
enormity of wearing man's attire. Religion had been
scandalised, and the Church horrified at such monstrosi-
ties; therefore it was decreed that she be delivered into
the hand of the executioner to receive the penalty of her
crimes, unless (for her enemies clung with desperate
tenacity to the hope she would give up her pretensions)
she would recant. A momentary pity seemed to have
touched the bystanders, not unmingled perhaps with
admiration for the noble girl standing there in the very
jaws of death. She was entreated to save herself—did
she wish to die? She had only to sign her name to a
few sentences, and the Church would keep possession of
her, and she might ultimately be restored to liberty. Is
it any marvel that these representations prevailed? Life
is sweet, and death is peculiarly repulsive to the young,
however it may be acquiesced in by the aged and the
wretched. If Cranmer gave way under similar circumstances, what may not be said in behalf of one so young
and so unsophisticated as the "Maiden from Lorraine!"

Jeanne expressed her readiness to recant. A small
document of six lines * was at once produced and handed
to her for signature. She blushed, for she had now to
confess her ignorance—her inability to sign her name.

* Afterwards published in *six pages*.

It was intimated to her that if she made a cross upon
the paper, it would be equally valid.   She did so, and
thus formally admitted the truth of the accusations
which had been brought against her.

The triumph of her enemies was now complete. They
had humbled and degraded her, had confused her with
abstruse questions, and alarmed her by spiritual terrors ;
they had broken her spirit with long imprisonment, and
it is even doubtful if she could have said with Francis I.,
" all is lost except our honour ;" and now they could
seek to justify themselves by a confession bearing her
own signature, that she was an impostor, if not something worse.

And now we have an illustration of the Christian
charity of that branch of the Church which knows so
well how to deal with heretics.   Jeanne's trial had been
purely ecclesiastical—a bishop was the chief judge, the
charges were of a spiritual character, relating to faith
and morals.   Otherwise she could not have been tried at
all ; for she was a prisoner of war, she owed no allegi-
ance to those into whose hands she had fallen ; and
although they might have put her to death, they knew
it would be an outrage of the laws of chivalry.   The
Church was therefore used as a means of condemning
her, and that succeeding, the secular power would have
been called in to finish the tragedy ; for the holy priest-
hood, though " exceedingly mad " against heresy, would
have exclaimed in pious horror, " It is not lawful for us
to put any man to death."   But Jeanne had not been
proved guilty ; she had confessed it as part of her required submission to the Church, and in hope of receiving
that mercy from her Church which she could not expect
at the hands of the English.

The bishop rose to pronounce sentence.   A solemn

stillness prevailed as these fearful words were heard: "Return, Jeanne, to the place from whence you came, there to be detained till death upon the bread of affliction and the water of affliction, for the recovery of thy soul."

The agony and horror of the unfortunate Maiden as she listened to this frightful sentence was depicted upon her countenance, but cannot be expressed in words. She clasped her hands despairingly, and for a moment her frame was convulsed. But as if weakness had been developed into strength, she suddenly became herself again, the woman was once more the heroine. She declared that she recanted her recantation, which had been forced from her, but which she now entirely and solemnly repudiated and recalled.

The rage of the soldiery was unbounded, while the judges were not a little chagrined. The assembly broke up in confusion, and with some amount of roughness Jeanne was conducted back to her prison. After she had retired to rest, her male costume was taken away, and she found herself the next day obliged to dress in ordinary female apparel. This was interpreted to mean submission to the Church, and an adhesion to the recantation to which she had put her hand; but on Trinity Sunday morning she found, on wishing to rise, that her female dress had been removed, and her old costume substituted. What was she to do? There was but one alternative, either to assume it or remain in bed. She chose the former, and thus sealed her fate; for all this was a deep design. A pretext was wanted for ensuring her destruction, and one that could neither be palliated nor condoned. And here was the very thing required. For heretics may (with difficulty) be pardoned, but the Church knows no mercy for those who relapse; and now it could be shown that Jeanne had fallen away from a state of repentance, and therefore from a state of grace, that her soul was possessed by the Evil one, and that nothing was gained by permitting her to live.

A matter so important was not to rest on trivial evidence. It is said that the Earl of Warwick and the Bishop of Beauvais were sent for, and hastened to the prison, where, from a secret standpoint, they witnessed the fact of her resumption of male attire.

The next day the bishop, accompanied by the inquisitor and eight assessors, visited the Maiden in her cell, and examined her as to this relapse. The inevitable necessity which had forced this act upon her had no weight in the opinion of her judges. As Pharaoh required the usual complement of bricks, whether the necessary straw were supplied or not, so the deprivation of a certain costume was no reason for not wearing it. She had been required, as a condition of life, not to appear again in her manly garb, and she was reminded that she had been taken in the very act of disobedience. This defiance of an ecclesiastical decree was a sin against the Church, proceeding from a perverse and rebellious disposition, which even Scripture declares to be " as the sin of witchcraft ; " and as she had thus set herself against the Church, the Church could no longer concern itself with her protection.

Jeanne's reply was healthy and fearless in its tone. She declared that she had put on the proscribed dress from the absence of any other, but she avowed her preference for it, and that she would rather die than remain any longer chained to the pillars of her prison.

As it could now be pleaded that she was a contumacious heretic and apostate, the bishop declared in council that it was necessary sentence of death should be pronounced. The necessity was a political one, and the attempt to give it a religious aspect was transparent in the extreme. Too often have the clergy given their countenance and support to political circumstances of this character; and religion has thus been imprudently and needlessly connected with some of the saddest episodes in History.

A confessor was sent to announce to the prisoner the mournful intelligence that she was to be burned alive! This burning alive has ever been a favourite mode of punishment with that Church which professes to belong to Him who was so meek and mild that He wept at even the sight of human suffering, and who declared it should be a characteristic of His people that they loved one another, and who forbade most strictly any display of malice even to an enemy. Burned alive! It was reserved for the Christian Church to initiate a mode of execution whose brutality is not surpassed by any of the recorded practices of heathenism.

This cruel announcement could not but produce in the victim the keenest anguish and despair. "Alas, alas!" cried Jeanne, "why do they treat me so horribly, so cruelly? Why must my body, so clean and pure, which has never been soiled with the least touch of corruption, be consumed and reduced to ashes? Oh, let me be beheaded seven times over rather than be burned! I appeal to God, my great Judge, against the injustice and tortures which I am made to suffer."

Having confessed, according to the requirements of the Church to which she belonged, Jeanne requested to be allowed to receive the holy communion. Common sense would have accepted this request as an evidence of Christian faith and a firm belief in existing Church membership. Consistency on the part of a Church which had condemned her to death on the ground that she was a heretic and an apostate would have refused compliance;

the bishop, however, consented on condition that it should be strictly private. But the clergy, to whom application was made for the necessary appliances, protested against what they considered a dishonour to the sacrament. They insisted that the holy elements should be accompanied with the usual procession and surroundings, and they prevailed. The eucharist was accordingly conveyed to the prison with a procession of clergy, who chanted the usual litanies, and called upon the spectators in the streets to "pray for her."

After communicating, she perceived the bishop, and said to him sorrowfully, "Bishop, I die through you."

The bishop retired with feelings that cannot be envied.

XIII.

THE TRAGEDY.

"Let me ever mourn
Thy early fate and too untimely urn,
In the full pride of youth thy glories fade,
And thou in ashes must with them be laid."—CONGREVE.

At nine o'clock on the morning of 30th May 1431, dressed in female costume, Jeanne ascended the executioner's car.

Rouen poured forth its inhabitants to witness a scene which was to render that city infamous for all time. English troops were assembled in sufficient numbers to repress any demonstration in the prisoner's favour. Jeanne had always expected deliverance ; she had more than once expressed her confident expectation of it. "My voices," she said on one occasion, "have told me that I shall be delivered from the English." Who then shall analyse her feelings at this awful moment! She found

herself deprived of her delegated character, disarmed by
her Church, deserted by her prince, denied by her people,
led to execution by those English, whom to defeat and
to drive out of her country she had assumed her mission.
What wonder, then, that the cry of agony escaped her lips,
" O Rouen, is it possible that I am to die here ? "

In the Old Market-place, now known as La Place de
la Pucelle, three scaffolds had been prepared. One of
these was occupied by the English cardinal and other pre-
lates who would not forego the sight of exquisite human
suffering. The second was for the use of the preacher
and the judges, for the mind of the sufferer was to be harassed by spiritual terrors as a kind of ecclesiastical vale-
diction. The third construction was an immense funeral
pile, whose gigantic appearance was enough to strike
terror into the hearts of the beholders.

The sermon, delivered by one of the most accomplished
preachers from the University of Paris, was founded
upon the text, " If one member suffer, all the members
suffer with it." To an unsophisticated mind it would
appear that no passage of Scripture could be more entirely
opposed to what was then being perpetrated. The text
implies that the members of the Christian Church are
connected together by such a sympathetic bond that the
interest of one is the interest of all, and that the happiness of all should be the endeavour of each. Therefore
that any who profess and call themselves Christians
should unite to persecute and consign to perdition one of
their number, must be in direct and palpable contraven-
tion of the spirit of the text. But the clerical mind is
no more bound by logic than the laws of the Church are
based upon charity. It was therefore argued that
Jeanne, hitherto a member of the Church, had sinned
grievously, that her sinful character and conduct had

caused much scandal and suffering to the Church at large, which was determined to get rid of her.

Before the sermon was concluded, Jeanne had fallen on her knees with her face buried in her hands. The attitude was one of deep and prayerful humiliation. The Bishop of Beauvais, with needless attention, called upon her to think only of her soul. Raising her head, her eyes filled with tears, she exclaimed, "Pray for me," and requested all present to pray for her. Some expressions are also reported which might bear the construction of a confession of sin, as if she had deceived and had been deceived, but as they rest only on English, and therefore hostile testimony, they are, to say the least, open to grave suspicion.

The bishop then rose to read her condemnation. He recounted the charges against her, and declared that she had been found guilty of idolatry, schism, intercourse with demons, and although admitted to penitence had wilfully relapsed, returning "like a dog to his vomit," and rendering fruitless all endeavours for her salvation. She was therefore cut off from the Church, as a withered branch is cut away for the safety and preservation of the tree; and as the destiny of such branches is to be burned, she was to be delivered over to the secular power, to be dealt with accordingly.

Cut away from all earthly hope and succour, the mind of the devoted Maiden mounted with sublime emotion to the only refuge of the soul in its supreme necessity. The crucified Redeemer, always precious, is never more so than when the earth is felt to be slipping away, and the soul feels itself to be on the confines of two worlds. She asked for a cross, the symbol of her faith, and two sticks were tied together and handed to her. She received it with respect, and placed it upon her breast, but her

friend, the monk Isambart, hastened to the Church of St
Saviour and obtained permission to take the crucifix
thence for her use. She then received her last confession,
and it is averred that this solemn office was interrupted
by the brutal impatience of the soldiery. At length they
seized her and led her to the pile. She shrunk in horror from the touch of the English, for whom she always
seems to have had great aversion. "O Rouen!" she
exclaimed, "wilt thou then be my last abode?"

Having been pinioned, she was bound to the stake,
and a mitre was placed upon her head, with this inscription: "Heretic, Relapsed, Apostate, Idolater."

Three hours had now elapsed since she left her
dungeon for this sad termination of her life and labours.
Hitherto she might have indulged the faint hope that the
expected deliverance would be vouchsafed. She might
have thought it incredible for her conscious integrity,
that a deed of such barbarity and injustice could be
really intended, but the appalling truth was now disclosed without the shadow of an uncertainty. As in
mountain travelling, the higher we ascend the more pure
we find the ether, the more extended the range of vision,
so there are heights in the soul's experience whence such
views are gained, and such ideas generated as could not
be conceived in the lowness and the littlenesses of
everyday life—

> " The dimness of my soul hath past,
> I see a better land at last;"

and thus it was with Jeanne. Although a shriek of
horror escaped her when the fire was first applied,
although she begged naturally for water, although all
possibility of deliverance had vanished, she was once
more the prophetess, the champion, the heroine, the

saint. "O Rouen!" she exclaimed, "I fear you will suffer for this." The Bishop of Beauvais, who seems to have been impelled by an uncontrollable impulse to confront his victim even to death, approached the pile as if to catch her last exclamations. She observed him, and said in a tone of calm reproach, "Bishop, I die through you."

And then came her solemn dying testimony to the truth of her mission. "No," she cried out, as if answering the suggestions of the tempter, "my voices have not deceived me." They had called her to the relief of Orleans, and she had relieved it; to the coronation of the Dauphin at Rheims, and it had been accomplished; to drive out the English from her country, and they were trembling for their possessions in Normandy. Her voices had prevented her deliverance, and here it was full and complete; sharp and painful indeed, but an apotheosis which was to render her memory immortal.

Two monks, whose sympathies seem to have been interested in her favour, and one of whom mounted the scaffold with her and remained till she begged him to retire for his own safety, have left this testimony on record: "We heard her invoke in the flames the saints, the archangel. She repeated the name of our Saviour; and lastly, her head falling, she repeated loudly, Jesus."

Was the triumph of the enemy then complete? Nothing indeed remained of the redoubtable Maiden but ashes, scarcely distinguishable from those of her funeral pyre. These were, by the command of the Cardinal of Winchester, collected and cast into the Seine, that no relic or remains might be left of her whose presence had once created homage, or inspired dread. But as the blood of her martyrs is the seed of the Church, so the perfidy and cruelty consummated at Rouen in the person of the hapless Maiden, rendered her one of the im-

perishable monuments in her nation's memory. The
enthusiastic gratitude of a people, of whom she was the
leader and great deliverer, may have invested her with
something of the miraculous, but the miracle consisted
in the utterly unselfish devotion which issued from an
ardent patriotism. For her country Jeanne lived, fought,
and died ; and though like a meteor, she seemed to vanish,
leaving a fiery track behind, posterity has acknowledged
that she was one of the noblest women whose names
adorn the pages of History. For benevolence of feeling,
sublimity of idea, purity of character, firmness of purpose,
moderation in the hour of triumph, patience in adversity,
submission to the Divine will, and inflexible faith in her
exalted mission, she seemed to be at once angel, woman,
virgin, soldier, and martyr.

> " A creature all too fair and good
> For human nature's daily food."

XIV.

CONCLUSION.

IT is not surprising that a career so extraordinary as that
of the " Maid of Orleans," bordering as it does upon the
marvellous, should have become the subject of "doubtful
disputations."

It has also had the misfortune incidental to mediæval
histories, to be entwined with circumstances which could
only have had their existence in the imagination of her
admirers. But after removing whatever excrescences
owe their origin to credulity, superstition, or enthusiastic panegyric, enough remains of this wondrous story, in
the opinion of those who have investigated it, to give it

a high place in the annals of History, and to make it the means of inculcating many lessons which have a tendency to elevate human nature. Two remarkable exceptions to this view, however, it is admitted, may be mentioned, Shakespeare, the genius of the English, and Voltaire of the French. It is strange that these two gifted and penetrating minds should have made the character of Jeanne Darc the butt of brutal and ribald jesting. For Shakespeare some excuse may be made. England had suffered dishonour and defeat through the agency of "her who was styled the Maid," and it is not easy to see virtue in an enemy. He wrote within a hundred years after Jeanne's memory and character had been honoured and rehabilitated by the pope, and at a time when England, in Protestant fervour, was in no mood to admire any papal proceedings. But for Voltaire there is no such extenuation. He was possessed with a love of mischief and power of destruction, "a great master of gibes and flouts and sneers." It has been said that the personage or institution upon which that "grinning skeleton" turned his sardonic smile and pointed his bony finger, sickened and withered under the baleful influence, and he knew his power and pushed it to extremes. But it is improbable that either Shakespeare or Voltaire concerned themselves in this matter about historical accuracy. They were poets; and poets, as Waller told our Charles II., only excel in fiction.*

The life and character of Jeanne Darc are attested by historical records whose authenticity is above suspicion.

The first reliable record to which we may refer is that of her trial at Rouen in A.D. 1431. It is owing to the information obtained in her answers at this trial that so

---

* Voltaire, for instance, represents Talbot as being taken prisoner at Orleans, whereas History tells us that Talbot was taken prisoner at Patay some weeks after Orleans was delivered.

much of her life is known. By this tribunal she was,
as we have seen, unjustly and cruelly condemned and
executed. When Charles, however, became master of
Rouen (1449), the first thing he did was to inquire into
the circumstances of this atrocious trial. He appointed
a commissary to collect evidence upon the subject, and
depositions were obtained from seven of those who had
assisted as assessors during her examination, and from
this evidence a memoir of the proceedings was drawn up
and submitted to the judgment of many doctors and
lawyers, who pronounced the judgment upon the Maid
to be invalid and unjust.

In 1452 the Cardinal Archbishop of Rouen (not
Cauchon, who had been disappointed in his hope of this
See), having inspected the documents and evidence thus
collected, proceeded, as pope's legate, to make an official
examination, when seventeen witnesses, selected principally from those who were engaged in the previous proceedings, were examined.

Charles being resolved that the character of the
heroine should be solemnly re-established, then applied
to Rome for a decree of rehabilitation. It was decided
that Jeanne's relations should present themselves and
make an appeal in their own names. Her father and
one of her brothers having died with grief for her cruel
death, the appeal was supported by her mother and two
surviving brothers, and accordingly, in June 1455, Pope
Calixtus III. issued authority to revise the process of
the condemnation at Rouen.

The tribunal appointed by this papal rescript assembled
in the archiepiscopal palace at Paris, and proceeded to
examine witnesses. Every person was summoned who
was supposed able to give evidence as to the facts.

A second inquiry was held at Orleans, a third at Paris,

and finally one at Rouen. All the testimony was concurrent in favour of the Maid, and accordingly, on the 7th July 1456, in the episcopal palace at Rouen, was pronounced the following decree, in the presence of the mother and brothers of Jeanne Darc, their counsel, and fourteen witnesses.

"The process, the abjuration, and the two judgments against Jeanne contain the most manifest fraud, injustice, and calumny, combined with errors in law and deed, and in consequence the whole is pronounced null and void."

MS. copies of these remarkable depositions may be seen in the public libraries of Paris and Geneva.*

An old MS. discovered at Orleans in 1818, has been ascertained to be an authentic document prepared by M. Giraut, who was a notary at Orleans from 1407 to 1439. In it reference is twice made to "Jehanne la Pucelle," and what she enabled the beleaguered town to do on the 4th May and the 8th May 1429.†

The MS. diary of the siege of Orleans, deposited to this day in the library at Orleans, is admitted to be genuine by the most reliable historians. It is full of minute details respecting the exploits of "this incomparable girl."

Jeanne had asked, as a reward for her services, that her birthplace might be free from all taxation. This was granted by the king in an ordinance, July 31, 1429, and again in 1459. It continued in force for three centuries. The registers of taxes for the election of Chaumont used, until the Revolution, to bear opposite the name of every village the sum to be received from it, but when they came to Domremy they always added, "Nothing, on account of the Maid." ‡

In Petitot's valuable collection of "Ancient Memoirs,"

---

* Quarterly Review, No. 69.
† "Jeanne Darc—A-t-elle existé?" published at Orleans.
‡ Quarterly Review, No. 69.

vol. viii., there are copies of unimpeachable documents testifying to the character and exploits of our heroine, notably the " Letter of the Count of Laval," in which he says, " The king sent for the Maid. She was armed at all points, save the head, and holding lance in hand. I went to her abode to see her. Wine was brought in, and she said to me she would soon give me some to drink in Paris. It is something divine to see her and to hear her. I saw her mount, armed all in white, save the head, a little axe in her hand, upon a great black courser, who would not at first let her mount him, then she said, ' Lead him to the cross which is before the church,' and then she mounted, without him so much as moving, and then she turned towards the church and said, ' You priests and churchmen make a procession and prayers to God.' To-day Monsieur d'Alençon, le bastard d'Orleans, and Goncourt, will set out from this place to go with La Pucelle. The king wishes to retain me with him till the Pucelle shall have been before the English forts at Orleans," etc.

Charles granted to her and her family, A.D. 1429, letters patent of nobility, with permission to use the lily as armorial bearings.* They assumed the surname of Du Lis.† A pension was also accorded to them by royal bounty. The family came to an end in the person of Messire Henri Francois de Coulouthe de Lys on the 29th June 1760, and with him expired the pension due in that quality. The city of Orleans granted a pension to the mother of Jeanne when she became a widow, and this pension was paid from the year 1438 until 1458, at which period she died at Orleans.

* The coat of arms is thus described: " Un Escu d'azur à une epée d'argent, le pommeau et la croisée d'or, soutenant sur la pointe une couronne d'or, avec deux fleurs-de-Lys d'or."
† Petitot, vol. viii.

A cross was erected, A.D. 1456, in the Old Market at Rouen, on the spot where the Maid had been burned. It is now replaced by a fountain, surmounted by a statue of her, and the place is denominated *La Place de la Pucelle*.

A solemn service is annually observed at Orleans on 8th May, to commemorate the assistance rendered to the city by their champion. It is customary on these occasions for some celebrated orator to pronounce a panegyric upon her character. The present Bishop of Orleans (Monsieur Dupanloup) has distinguished himself in this particular, and his orations will repay perusal. He has also taken steps to procure at Rome the canonisation of this patriotic martyr.

It is evident, therefore, from ancient MS., historical monuments, and the references to this event by the most reliable historians, that the general outline of the career of Jeanne Darc is authentic and veracious. It may be too much to affirm that she did or said all that has been ascribed to her; but that such a person did really assume a divine mission, that she headed the French troops on several occasions, and by the enthusiasm which she inspired, gave unexpected deliverance to Orleans and success to the cause of Charles VII., can only be denied by denying the possibility of authentic history.

But while there can be no question as to her life, there has been considerable questioning as to her death. And this has arisen from two circumstances: (1.) The apparent incredibility that Charles would have made no effort to avert it; and (2.) That a person pretending to be the Maid appeared at Metz a few years afterwards, and was recognised by Jeanne's two brothers, and subsequently on two occasions by the people of Orleans.

All the French historians, with one exception (M. Laverdy), attest that Charles made no exertion to save

her to whom he mainly owed his crown and kingdom.
His character and disposition at that time were feeble
and lethargic, and gave no promise of that energy which,
in after years, procured him the title of VICTORIOUS. It
was with difficulty he was persuaded to grant the Maid
an interview, to accept her services, to march to Rheims;
but he had no difficulty in making the repulse at Paris
an excuse for shameful retreat and still more shameful
sloth. We may well ask why he did not negotiate for
her ransom, and we may wonder at his ingratitude, but
the case, alas, is one to which History can furnish too
many parallels. When the noble Wallace was taken
prisoner by Edward I., no efforts seem to have been
made by the Scots to ransom or release their hero.

The French king, John, taken prisoner by our own
Black Prince, was suffered to languish and die in captivity, neither his family, his nobles, nor his people
making an effort to release him.

The beautiful and unfortunate Mary Queen of Scots
was imprisoned and executed by order of Elizabeth, and
no serious effort to save her was made either by her
subjects or by her son, who was then James VI. of
Scotland.

If ever a devoted servant deserved well of his
sovereign, the Earl of Strafford had strong claims upon
Charles I. The fate of that unhappy nobleman, however, adds another illustration to the well-known adage
as to the ingratitude of kings.

The appearance of a personage who pretended to be
the real Maid of Orleans is an authenticated fact of
history. Nine years after Jeanne's well-attested death,
it is stated a woman was presented to Charles assuming
the name of La Pucelle; but she soon confessed the fraud,
and was pardoned.

On the 20th May 1436, a pretended Pucelle made her appearance at Metz, was recognised by Jeanne's two brothers, and also by the city of Orleans. She travelled to Cologne, afterwards espoused Sir Robert des Armoisies, but did not present herself at Court.

There is nothing surprising in the mere fact that a career so extraordinary, ending in a fate so tragical, caused Jeanne to be impersonated after death, or that such imposture found ready credence among a people so excitable and sensitive. And here again history affords illustrations. The two young princes who were murdered in the Tower at the instance of Richard III. furnish a case in point. Perkin Warbeck, in the reign of Henry VII., pretended to be one of the unfortunate princes. He declared himself to be the Duke of York, and his claims were allowed and his cause espoused by such high authorities as the Duchess of Burgundy and the King of Scotland. In the same reign a person of mean extraction, named Lambert Simnel, pretended to be the Earl of Warwick, who was then, and had been for many years, a close prisoner in the Tower, and although the king produced the real earl in refutation of the imposture, it did not prevent Simnel from obtaining such support that he was enabled to attack the royal forces. Less than two years ago the claims of a person assuming to be a lineal descendant of the Dauphin of France, who perished in the first Revolution, occupied the attention of a French tribunal, which declared the claims unfounded. To this day the rights of a person who claimed to be the long lost heir of the Tichborne estates are believed in by great numbers of the English working classes, and this belief receives no small justification from the circumstance that the impostor was acknowledged as her son by the mother of the missing heir.

In the case of the pretended Maid of Orleans, the only
circumstance in her favour is the recognition of her
claims by Jeanne's two brothers. Granting, as we must,
that the pretender strongly resembled the martyred
Maiden, we can understand the readiness with which
the good people of Orleans received her, their joy at her
supposed escape, their enthusiastic welcome and rejoic-
ing. It was six years since they had seen her, and they
were only too ready to believe what they ardently hoped
might be true. But it is difficult in the highest degree
to explain away the fact that the two brothers of Jeanne
acknowledged the pretender to be their sister. That
they could have been really deceived by a stranger palm-
ing herself off as their sister, with whom they had been
in social intercourse but six years previously, seems beyond the region of probability.

That Jeanne was really condemned to die is proved by
indisputable evidence.* That some one was burned at
Rouen purporting to be the Maid of Orleans is equally
certain. If Jeanne was not really burned, somebody was
substituted for her, and if she regained her liberty it
could only be by the connivance of her gaolers. It is
difficult to conceive what advantage was to be gained
from pretending to execute the Maid, and then permitting
her to escape and expose the pretence. Why should the
English have incurred such expense and pains to possess
themselves of her person, to subject her to long imprisonment and a grievous trial, to find her guilty of witchcraft
and heresy, and then to let her go free? Would she not
have gone to the king, if she escaped, where she would
have been sure of a joyous reception? But the pretender
went to Metz, and appears *never* to have been received
at Court. Nor does it appear that she was ever recog-

* Procès de Condamnation, etc., Paris.

nised or acknowledged by Jeanne's mother, who to the
day of her death received a pension from the city of
Orleans as a tribute to her daughter's services and
memory. Why should the king have been at such
trouble to reverse the decision against her when the
fact of her being set at liberty sufficiently refuted the
charges? Why should a cross have been erected at
Rouen to mark the place of her execution if Jeanne
were really living to testify that no such execution took
place? Why did King Henry VI. write to the Duke of
Burgundy and to several European Courts an account of
her trial, condemnation, and *execution*, knowing that
such execution had not taken place, and that the pretended victim was at large to convict him of falsehood?
Why should English historians have admitted the fact,
and allowed their countrymen to lie under the stigma of
so base a crime, if it had really not been perpetrated?
Upwards of a century ago it was computed that more
than eighty reliable French writers had given accounts
of the career of the Maid of Orleans, and their testimony
is concurrent as to her tragical end.* And, finally, what
are we to say to the testimony on oath of each of the
two monks who were present at her execution, who had
attended her in prison, and who, having nothing to hope
from the propagation of a falsehood, solemnly affirmed
that they were eye-witnesses of her death?

It may be interesting to know that the cruelty of
which Jeanne had been the victim recoiled upon those
who were mainly responsible. The English were dispos-
sessed of their acquisitions in France, except Calais; †
Henry VI. was harassed by the Wars of the Roses,
and died a prisoner in the Tower, not without suspi-

* Bibliotheque de la France, tome ii.
† Which they lost in the reign of Mary.

cion of violence; Cauchon, the malignant bishop, des-
pised and disliked, died of apoplexy; the Cardinal of
Winchester died in 1448, leaving behind him the following character: "He was descended of an honourable
lineage, but born in haste, more noble in blood than
notable in learning, haughty in stomach and high of
countenance, rich above measure but not very liberal,
disdainful to his kin and dreadful to his lovers, prefer-
ring money before friendship, many things beginning
and few performing saving in malice and mischief, his
insatiable covetousness and hope of long life made him
both to forget God, his prince, and himself."[*] Estivet
the proctor was found dead in a dovecot; Nicholas Midi
died of a leprosy; De Flavy was strangled; and Bedford
the regent died at Rouen, in the very castle which contained the dungeon in which the ill-requited Maiden had
been immured.

Deposited in the Imperial Library at Paris is an
ancient MS., believed to have been prepared at Rouen,
1465, by one of those who had acted as assessors at the
trial, in which he gives a quaint device for remembering
the date of the Maiden's martyrdom. By extracting the
numerals which are so printed as to catch the eye, they
will be found to make up the year 1431:

"sVb HenrICo regnante In FranCIa
CoMbVsta fVIt InIVsto pVeLLa."

* Hollinshed, vol. iii.

THE COUNTESS OF NITHSDALE.

WINNIFRED, COUNTESS OF NITHSDALE, was the youngest daughter of the Marquis of Powis; and it is said that she was contracted in marriage, by her mother, to Lord Nithsdale, without being consulted, and even before she had seen him. If this statement be correct, the sweetness and willing obedience with which she submitted was rewarded by so warm and mutual an affection in married life that it made the happiness of many tranquil years, and in the end, when trial and sorrow came, prompted her to an act of courage and daring, in which love alone could have sustained her.

Actuated by serious personal and political convictions, Lord Nithsdale joined the unfortunate Scottish rebellion in 1715. It is unnecessary to detail here the progress of this ill-fated scheme. Enough to state that it ended in disastrous defeat, and the imprisonment of those principally concerned. Lord Nithsdale, Lord Derwentwater, and other Scottish noblemen, were tried in London, and condemned to death as traitors. Lady Nithsdale, when the news of her husband's imprisonment reached her, was residing at her home in Peeblesshire in the south of Scotland; and hearing that he had expressed an earnest desire to see her, she, without hesitation, resolved to set out for the metropolis. It was in the depth of winter, and the roads were nearly impassable, but she succeeded, through great difficulties, in reaching Newcastle, and from thence proceeded to York by the ordinary stage-coach. At the

latter place the increased severity of the weather, and
the depth of the snow, would not admit of the stage proceeding farther, and even the mails were detained; but
the errand of Lady Nithsdale was one from which no
risks could deter her.   She therefore pursued her way on
horseback, though the snow frequently was so deep that
it encumbered the animal she rode above its saddle-girths.
At length, however, she reached London; and, supported
both in health and spirits by unfaltering love and firm
resolution, she suffered no ill effects from her perilous
journey.

On arriving at the Tower, where her husband was
confined, she found to her dismay that she could not be
permitted to see him unless she would consent to become
a prisoner with him.   This she refused to do, as it would
prevent her acting in her husband's behalf by securing
the assistance and intercession of friends, and, above all,
by submitting to imprisonment she would be prevented
from carrying out a plan of escape which she had already
formed should her worst apprehensions prove to be true.
She therefore refused to submit to such a condition, assign-
ing as a reason that the state of her health prevented
her from enduring any degree of confinement.   She succeeded, however, in bribing the guard, and obtained frequent
interviews with her husband up to the day on which the
prisoners were condemned; after which, for the last week,
their families were allowed free access to take a last leave
of them.

Immediately on her arrival in London, Lady Nithsdale began to labour on behalf of the life of her husband,
making application to all persons in authority, wherever
there was even the most remote chance of receiving any
assistance; but from most of those in power she only
obtained assurances that her cause was hopeless, and that

for particular reasons her husband was certain to be executed. Lord Nithsdale, more for his wife's sake than for his
own, agreed to a petition being presented to the king on
his behalf; trusting, by this means, to excite for her his
sympathy and indulgence. It was well-known that the
king was especially incensed against Nithsdale, so that he
is said to have forbidden that any petition should be
presented, or address made for his pardon or release; but
his wife, in obedience to his wish, resolved to make the
attempt, and accordingly repaired to court.

In a narrative written to her sister, on the escape of
her husband, she thus recounts her interview with the
king, George I.:—

"So the first day that I heard the king was to go to
the drawing-room, I dressed myself in black, as if I had
been in mourning, and sent for Mrs. Morgan (the same
who accompanied me to the Tower); because, as I did not
know his majesty personally, I might have mistaken some
other person for him. She stayed by me, and told me
when he was coming. I had another lady with me, and
we remained in a room between the king's apartments
and the drawing-room, so that he was obliged to go
through it; and, as there were three windows in it, we
sat in the middle one, that I might have time enough to
meet him before he could pass. I threw myself at his
feet, and told him in French, that I was the unfortunate
Countess of Nithsdale, that he might not pretend to be
ignorant of my person. But perceiving that he wanted
to go off without receiving my petition, I caught hold of
the skirt of his coat, that he might stop and hear me.
He endeavoured to escape out of my hands, but I kept
such strong hold, that he dragged me on my knees from
the middle of the room to the very door of the drawing-
room. At last one of the blue ribbons who attended his

majesty, took me round the waist, while another wrested
the coat out of my hands. The petition, which I had
endeavoured to thrust into his pocket, fell down in the
souffle, and I almost fainted away through grief and disappointment. One of the gentlemen in waiting picked
up the petition; and, as I knew that it ought to have
been given to the lord of the bedchamber, who was then
in waiting, I wrote to him, and entreated him to do me
the favour to read the petition which I had had the
honour to present to his majesty. Fortunately for me it
happened to be my Lord Dorset, with whom Mrs. Mor-
gau was very intimate. Accordingly she went into the
drawing-room and delivered him the letter, which he
received very graciously. He could not read it then, as
he was at cards with the Prince; but as soon as ever the
game was over he read it, and behaved (as I afterwards
learned) with the warmest zeal for my interest, and was
seconded by the Duke of Montrose, who had seen me in
the antechamber, and wanted to speak to me. But I
made him a sign not to come near me, lest his acquaintance might thwart my designs. They read over the
petition several times, but without any success; but it
became the topic of their conversation for the rest of the
evening, and the harshness with which I had been treated
soon spread abroad, not much to the honour of the king."

The only effect produced by this painful scene seems
to have been an acceleration of the preparations for the
execution; for on the following Friday (the petition had
been presented on Monday) it was decided in council that
the sentence against the condemned noblemen should be
carried into effect.

In the meantime Lady Derwentwater and other ladies
of rank were strenuous in their endeavours to prevent the
execution of the sentence. They succeeded in obtaining

an interview with the king, which, however, proved futile. They also attended at both Houses of Parliament to present petitions to the members as they went in. These petitions had a decided influence. In the Commons a motion to petition the king in favour of the unfortunate noblemen was lost by only seven votes; and among the Lords a still stronger personal feeling and interest was excited, but all proved unavailing; and Lady Nithsdale, after joining with the other ladies in this ineffectual attendance, at length found that all her hope and dependence must rest on her long-formed scheme of bringing about her husband's escape. She had less than twenty-four hours to arrange everything, and to persuade accomplices to aid her in her hazardous project. In all these she was extremely fortunate; her story is best told in her own words:—

"As the motion had passed generally (that the petitions should be read in the Lords, which had only been carried after a warm debate), I thought I would draw some advantage in favour of my design. Accordingly, I immediately left the House of Lords, and hastened to the Tower, where, affecting an air of joy and satisfaction, I told all the guards I passed that I came to bring joyful tidings to the prisoner. I desired them to lay aside their fears, for the petition had passed the House in his favour. I then gave them some money to drink to the lords and his majesty, though it was but trifling, for I thought that if I were too liberal on the occasion they might suspect my designs, and that giving them something would gain their good humour and services for the next day, which was the eve of the execution. The next morning I could not go to the Tower, having so many things on my hands to put in readiness; but in the evening, when all was ready, I sent for Mrs. Mills, with whom I lodged, and

acquainted her with my design of attempting my lord's
escape, as there was no prospect of his being pardoned,
and this was the last night before the execution. I told
her that I had everything in readiness, and that I
trusted she would not refuse to accompany me, that
my lord might pass for her. I pressed her to come
immediately, as we had no time to lose. At the
same time I sent for Mrs. Morgan, then usually known
by the name of Hilton, to whose acquaintance my
dear Evans (her maid) had introduced me; which I
looked upon as a very singular happiness. I immediately communicated my resolution to her. She was
of a very tall and slender make, so I begged her to
put on under her own riding-hood one that I had prepared for Mrs. Mills, as she was to lend hers to my lord,
that in coming out he might be taken for her. When we
were in the coach I never ceased talking, that they might
have no leisure to reflect. Their surprise and astonishment when I first opened my design to them had made
them consent, without ever thinking of the consequences.

"On our arrival at the Tower, the first person I introduced was Mrs. Morgan, for I was only allowed to take
in one at a time. Mrs. Morgan brought with her the
clothes which were to serve Mrs. Mills when she left her
own behind her. When Mrs. Morgan had taken off what
she had brought for my purpose, I conducted her back to
the staircase; and, in going, I asked her to send in my maid
to dress me: that I was afraid of being too late to present
my petition that night, if she did not come immediately.
I despatched her safe, and went partly down-stairs to
meet Mrs. Mills, who had the precaution to hold her
handkerchief to her face, as was very natural for a woman
to do when she was going to bid her last farewell to a
friend on the evening of his execution. I had, indeed,

desired her to do it, that my lord might go out in the same manner. I also bought an artificial head-dress of sandy-coloured hair, and I painted my husband's face white, and put rouge upon his cheeks, so as to hide his long beard, which he had not had time to shave. All this provision I had before left in the Tower.

"The poor guards, whom my liberality the day before had endeared me to, let me go quietly with my company, and were not so strictly on the watch as they had hitherto been; and the more so as they were persuaded from what I had told them the day before that the prisoners would obtain their pardon. I made Mrs. Mills take off her own hood, and put on that which I had brought for her. I then took her by the hand, and led her out of my lord's chamber, and in passing through the next room, in which there were several people, with all the concern imaginable I said, 'My dear Mrs. Catherine, go in all haste, and send me my waiting-maid; she certainly cannot reflect how late it is; she forgets that I am to present a petition to-night, and if I let slip this opportunity I am undone, for to-morrow will be too late. Hasten her as much as possible, for I shall be on thorns till she comes.' Every person in the room, who were chiefly the wives and daughters of the guards, seemed to compassionate me exceedingly, and the sentinel officiously opened the door.

"When I had seen her out I returned back to my lord, and finished dressing him. I had taken care that Mrs. Mills did not go out crying, as she came in, that my lord might the better pass for the lady who came in crying and afflicted; and the more so because he had the same dress she wore. When I had dressed my husband in all my petticoats except one, I perceived that it was growing dark, and was afraid that the light of the candles might betray us, so I resolved to set off. I went out leading

him by the hand, and he held his handkerchief to his
eyes. I spoke to him and in the most piteous and afflicted
tone of voice, bewailing bitterly the negligence of Evans,
who had ruined me by her delay. Then said I: 'My
dear Mrs. Betty, for the love of God run quickly and
bring her with you. You know my lodging, and if ever
you made despatch in your life, do it at present. I am
distracted with this disappointment.' The guards opened
the doors, and I went down-stairs with him, still urging
all possible despatch. As soon as he had cleared the door,
I made him walk before me, lest the sentinel should take
notice of his walk; but I still continued to press him to
make all the despatch he possibly could. At the bottom
of the stairs I met my dear Evans, into whose hands I
confided him.[1]

"I had before engaged Mr. Mills to be in readiness
before the Tower to conduct him to some place in safety,
in case he succeeded. He looked upon the whole affair
as so very improbable to succeed, that his astonishment
when he saw us nearly deprived him of his senses, which
Evans perceiving, with the greatest presence of mind
without telling him (Lord Nithsdale) anything, lest he
should mistrust them, conducted him to some of her own
friends, on whom she could rely, and so secured him;
without which we should have been undone. When she
had conducted him and left him with them, she returned
to find Mr. Mills, who by this time had recovered from
his astonishment. They went home together, and having
found a place of security they conducted him to it.

"In the meantime, as I had pretended to have sent the
young lady on an errand, I was obliged to return upstairs

---

[1] It will be observed that though only three persons entered the apartment of
Lord Nithsdale, four were allowed to leave it. From the fact of all being
dressed as women, the guards must have either become careless, or become confused.

and go back to my lord's room in the same feigned anxiety
of being too late; so that everybody seemed entirely to
sympathize with my distress. When I was in the room,
I talked to him as if he had been really present, and
answered my own questions in my husband's voice, as
nearly as I could imitate it. I walked up and down, as
if we were conversing together, till I thought they had
time enough thoroughly to clear themselves of the guards.
I then thought proper to make off also. I opened the
door, and stood half in it, that those in the outward
chamber might hear what I said, but held it so close that
they could not look in. I bade my lord a formal farewell
for that night, and added that something more than usual
must have happened to make Evans negligent on this
important occasion, as I had always found her so punctual
even in the most trifling matters; that if the Tower was
still open when I had finished my business I would return
for the night, but that he might be assured that I would
be with him as early in the morning as I could gain
admittance to the Tower; and I flattered myself I should
bring favourable news. Then, before I shut the door, I
pulled the string through the latch, so that it could only
be opened on the inside. I then shut it with some degree
of force, that I might be sure of its being well shut. I
said to the servant as I passed by (who was ignorant of
the whole transaction) that he need not carry coals in to
his master until my lord sent for him, as he desired to
finish some prayers first. I went down-stairs and called
a coach; I then was driven to my lodgings, where poor
Mr. Mackenzie had been waiting to carry the petition in
case my attempt failed. I told him there was no need of
any petition, as my lord was safe out of the Tower, and
out of the hands of his enemies, but that I did not know
where he was.

"I discharged the coach and sent for a sedan-chair, and
went to the Duchess of Buccleuch, who expected me
about that time, as I had begged of her to present the
petition for me, having taken my precautions against all
events.   I asked if she was at home, and they answered
that she expected me, and had another duchess with her.
I refused to go upstairs as she had company, and I was
not in a condition to be introduced to strangers.   I begged
to be shown into a chamber below stairs, and that they
would have the goodness to send her grace's maid to me,
having something to say to her.   I had discharged the
chair, lest I should be pursued and watched.   When the
maid came in, I desired her to present my most humble
respects to her grace, and to say that I did not care to
come upstairs because she had company with her.   I also
charged her with my sincerest thanks for her kind offer to
accompany me when I went to present my petition.   I
added that she might spare herself any further trouble, as
it was now judged more advisable to present one general
petition in the name of all; however, that I should never
be unmindful of my particular obligations to her grace,
which I would return very soon to acknowledge in person.

"I then desired one of the servants to call a chair, and
I went to the Duchess of Montrose, who had always borne
a part in my distresses.   When I arrived, she left her
company to deny herself, not being able to see me
under the affliction which she judged me to be in.   By
mistake, however, I was admitted, so there was no remedy.
She came to me, and, as my heart was in an ecstasy of
joy, I expressed it in my countenance as she entered the
room.   I ran up to her in the transport of my joy.   She
appeared to be exceedingly shocked and frightened, and
afterwards confessed to me that she apprehended my

trouble had thrown me out of my self, till I communicated my happiness to her. She then advised me to retire to some place of security, for that the king was highly displeased, and even enraged, at the petition I had presented to him, and had complained of it severely. I sent for another chair; for I always discharged them immediately, lest I might be pursued. Her grace said she would go to court, and see how the news of my lord's escape would be received. When the news was brought to the king he flew into a violent passion, and said he was betrayed, for it could not have been done without some confederacy. He instantly despatched two persons to the Tower, to see that the other prisoners were secure, lest they should follow the example.

"When I left the duchess, I went to a house which Evans had found out for me, and where she promised to inform me where my husband was. She got thither some few minutes after me, and told me that, when she had seen him secure, she went in search of Mr. Mills, who by this time had recovered from his astonishment; that he returned to her house, where she had found him, and that he had removed my lord from the first place where she had desired them to wait, to the house of a poor woman directly opposite to the guard-house. She had but one small room, up a flight of stairs, and a very small bed in it. We threw ourselves upon the bed, that we might not be heard walking up or down. She left us a bottle of wine and some bread, and Mrs. Mills brought us some more in her pocket next day. We subsisted on this provision from Thursday to Saturday night, when Mrs. Mills came and conducted my lord to the house of the Venetian ambassador. We did not communicate the affair to his excellency, but one of his servants concealed him in his own room till Wednesday, on which day the

ambassador's coach and six was to go down to Dover to
meet his brother. My lord put on a livery, and went
down in the retinue, without the least suspicion, to
Dover, when M. Michel (which was the name of the
ambassador's servant) hired a small vessel, and immediately set sail for Calais. This passage was so remarkably
short, that the captain threw out this reflection, that the
wind could not have served better if his passengers had
been flying for their lives, little thinking it to be really
the case.

"For my part, I absconded to the house of an honest
man in Drury Lane, where I remained till I was assured
of my lord's safe arrival on the Continent. I then wrote
to the Duchess of Buccleuch (everybody thought till then
that I had gone off with my husband) to tell her that I
understood I was suspected of having contrived my lord's
escape, as was very natural to suppose; that, if I could
have been happy enough to have done it, I should be
flattered to have the merit of it attributed to me; but
that a bare suspicion, without proof, could never be a
sufficient ground for my being punished for a supposed
offence, though it might be motive enough for me to
provide a place of security; so I entreated her to procure
leave for me to go with safety about my business. So far
from granting my request, they were resolved to secure
me, if possible. After several debates, the solicitor-
general, who was an utter stranger to me, had the
humanity to say that, since I showed so much respect for
government as not to appear in public, it would be cruel
to make any search for me; upon which, it was decided
that, if I remained concealed, no further search would be
made; but that if I appeared, either in England or Scotland, I should be secured."

Lady Nithsdale felt, however, that more was yet to be

done, and that the poor indulgence which had been granted to her was not sufficient, unless she would submit to expose her children to beggary.

On first hearing of her husband's apprehension, she had thought it prudent to conceal many important family papers and other valuables, and having no person at hand with whom they could be safely trusted, had hid them underground, in a place known only to the gardener, in whom she had great confidence. It proved a happy precaution, for, after her departure, the house had been searched, and, as she expressed it, "God only knows what might have transpired from these papers." In addition to the danger of their being discovered, there was the imminent risk of their being destroyed by damp, so that no time must be lost in removing them to a place of greater safety before it was too late. She therefore determined to take a journey to the north, and, for greater secrecy, on horseback, though this mode of travelling, which was new to her, was extremely fatiguing. She, however, with her maid Evans, and a servant who could be depended on, set out from London, and reached Traquair in Scotland in safety, and without any one being aware of her intentions. Here she ventured to rest for two days in the society of her sister-in-law and Lord Traquair, feeling security in the conviction that, as the lord lieutenant of the county was an old friend of her husband, he would not allow any search to be made after her without first giving her warning. From thence she proceeded to Terreagles, whither it was supposed she came with permission of the government, and, to keep up that opinion, she invited her neighbours to visit her. That same night she dug up the papers from their hiding-place, where happily they had sustained no injury, and sent them at once by safe hands to Traquair. This was accomplished just in time, for the magistrates of Dumfries began to entertain suspicions of her right to be there, and desired to have a sight of her authority. On hearing this, as she writes in her narrative, "I expressed my surprise that they had been so backward in paying their respects; but, said I, better late than never: be sure to tell them that they will be welcome whenever they choose to come. This was after dinner; but I lost no time to put everything in readiness, doing this with all possible secrecy; but the next morning, before daybreak, I set off again for London with the same attendants, and as before, I put up at the smallest inns, and arrived safe once more."

George I. could not forgive Lady Nithsdale for the heroic part she had acted; he refused in her case the allowance or dower which was granted to the wives of the other lords. "A lady informed me," she wrote, "that the king was greatly incensed at the news of my lord's escape—that he had issued orders to have me arrested, adding that I did whatever I pleased, despite of all his designs—and that I had given him more trouble than any woman in all Europe. For which reason I kept myself as close concealed as possible, till the heat of these rumours had abated. In the meanwhile, I took the opinion of a very famous lawyer, who was a man of the strictest probity. He advised me to go off as soon as they had ceased searching for me. I followed his advice, and about a fortnight after I escaped without any accident whatever."

Lady Nithsdale met her husband and children at Paris, whither they had come from Bruges to receive her.

After this wonderful escape, Lord Nithsdale lived nearly thirty years, and died at Rome in 1744. His wife survived him five years. She had the satisfaction of having provided a competency for her son by her hazardous journey to Scotland, though the title and principal estates had been confiscated by the attainder of his father.

FLORA MACDONALD.

AFTER the disastrous battle of Culloden in 1746, Prince Charles Edward Stuart took refuge in the western islands of Scotland, whence he hoped to make his escape to France. The whole force of the government was spread about in pursuit of him, and a reward of £30,000 was offered for his capture. As he was known to be concealed amongst a poor and destitute population, it was not supposed possible but that the prospect of boundless wealth should influence some one to communicate the place of his retreat; but in this expectation the simple loyalty of the Highland clans, and their sense of the duties of hospitality had not been sufficiently considered, and for days and weeks the hapless prince wandered among these devoted people, enduring extremities of hardship, but in greater security, probably, than any other spot in the kingdom of his fathers could have afforded him.

The battle of Culloden was fought on the 15th of April, and the prince having made his escape at once from the mainland, he wandered for two months among the hills and moors of Benbecula, South Uist, and the smaller neighbouring isles, accompanied by a few Highland gentlemen, who shared with him his troubles and dangers. It was on learning that a body of men, numbering five hundred, were landed on South Uist, and were within a mile and a half of him, that the separation and immediate flight of the party was agreed upon as absolutely necessary.

Prince Charles at that time was eminently qualified to attach his adherents. His youth and noble bearing, his courage in danger, his patience and cheerfulness under every difficulty, his consideration for those around him, and the freedom of intercourse which he encouraged, all combined with the hardships they shared in common to endear him to them.

When his friends had left him, the prince, accompanied only by his faithful attendants, Captain O'Neil, and Neil Mackechan, ascended a high hill in South Uist, from which he could command a view of the party sent in pursuit of him, and having remained there till nightfall, set out with his two companions on a toilsome march towards Benbecula, which was now thought a safer refuge. It was at this critical point of his wanderings that the prince received the assistance of Flora Macdonald, the details of which we shall here briefly narrate.

Flora, who at this time is described as a young and beautiful girl, was the daughter of Mr. Macdonald of Milton, in South Uist. On his death her mother had married again Hugh Macdonald, of Armadale, in the Isle of Skye, with whom Flora usually resided; but at this time she was on a visit with her brother in South Uist, and was on terms of intimacy with certain ladies of the island, Lady Clanronald, and Lady Margaret Macdonald, who had already shown much zeal in the service of Prince Charles.

Captain O'Neil, the companion of the prince, was previously well acquainted with Flora Macdonald, and was her warm though hopeless admirer, and whatever the circumstances may have been which led to her being concerned in this adventure, Captain O'Neil willingly undertook Charles' mission to seek an interview with her, and engage her assistance, either to accompany the prince

H

in his hazardous flight, or to concert with them the best
means for his escape.

An eminent writer on the subject [1] gives Captain
O'Neil's own account of his first interview with Miss
Macdonald.   He says:—

"At midnight we came to a hut, where, by good fortune, we met with Miss Flora Macdonald, whom I
formerly knew.   I quitted the prince at some distance
from the hut, and went with a design to inform myself if
the independent companies were to pass that way next
day.   The young lady answered me no, and said they were
not to pass till the day after.   Then I told her I had
brought a friend to see her, and she, with some emotion,
asked me if it was the prince.   I answered her it was, and
instantly brought him in.   We then consulted on the
imminent danger the prince was in, and could think of no
more proper and safe expedient than to propose to Miss
Flora to convey him to the Isle of Skye, where her mother
lived.   This seemed the more feasible, as the young lady's
step-father, being captain of an independent company,
would accord her a pass for herself and a servant, to go
and visit her mother.   The prince assented, and immediately proposed it to the young lady, to which she
answered with the greatest respect and loyalty, but
declined it, saying Sir Alexander Macdonald (husband of
Lady Margaret) was too much her friend for her to be the
instrument of his ruin.   I endeavoured to obviate this by
answering her that Sir Alexander was not in the country,
and that she could with the greatest facility convey the
prince to her mother's, as she lived close by the water-
side.   I then demonstrated to her the honour and immor-
tality that would redound to her by such a glorious action,
and she at length acquiesced, after the prince had told her

---

[1] Robert Chambers, LL.D. : *History of the Scottish Rebellions.*

the sense he would always retain of so conspicuous a service. She promised to acquaint us next day, when things were ripe for execution, and we parted for the mountains of Coradale," having previously agreed to send Neil Mackechan to arrange with her the details of the prince's escape.

The best road to Skye from South Uist was through the island of Benbecula—at low water connected with South Uist by a line of sand, but at other times communicated with by a ford or ferry, over which Miss Macdonald and Mackechan had to pass separately to their place of rendezvous. On nearing Benbecula Mackechan found himself, to his great dismay, in the midst of a body of Skye militia, who were strictly guarding the ford. From this it was evident that the unfortunate prince had been traced to South Uist. Imperative orders had been given that no one should pass the ford without first being taken to the guard-house, to be examined there by the commanding officer. Pursuant to this order Mackechan was conveyed to the guard-house, where, to his surprise, he found Miss Macdonald and her maid, who, being unprovided with passports, had also been detained in custody.

After her interview with the prince, Miss Macdonald had at once set about arranging the plan of his escape, and had succeeded in communicating by a trusty messenger with Lady Clanronald, of Ormaclade, with whom she had already concerted the plan, and provided that a small boat should be in readiness to convey him from Benbecula to Skye; and it was further arranged that he should assume a female dress, and under the name of Betty Burke pass for the maid of Miss Macdonald. She was now on her way to Lady Clanronald's house, to prepare with her the necessary articles for the disguise of the prince, when she was thus taken prisoner by the militia.

Her first inquiry on her detention, was for the name of the commandant, who proved, to her great satisfaction, to be her own step-father, Macdonald of Armadale. She was informed that he was absent at present, but would return on the following morning. To this unfortunate hindrance she resigned herself with apparent composure, and passed the night in the guard-house.

Her step-father came next morning, and to make up for the delay she had had to endure at so critical a time, she now obtained a passport for Neil Mackechan and Betty Burke, her maid, in whose favour he also provided her with the following letter to his wife, her mother:—

"I have sent your daughter from this country, lest she should be any way frightened with the troops lying here. She has got one Betty Burke, an Irish girl, who, as she tells me, is a good spinster. If her spinning please you, you may keep her till she spins all you want; or, if you have any wool to spin, you may employ her. I have sent Neil Mackechan also with your daughter and Betty Burke to take care of them. I am, your dutiful husband,

"HUGH MACDONALD."

Having succeeded thus far, Flora Macdonald despatched Mackechan in haste to conduct the prince without delay to Rossinish, where she would join them as soon as possible with the disguise, and the necessary requirements for the expedition. Neil made the best of his way back to the prince, whom he found still concealed in his wretched hiding-place among the rocks. The presence of the militia made it impossible to attempt passing the ford to Benbecula; it was therefore necessary to make their way thither from another point by sea. Unable to procure a boat, they happily espied a fishing yawl passing, and easily pre-

vailed upon its crew to land them on the opposite coast.
Rossinish, the place of rendezvous, was still far off, and
to reach it they had to pass through a bleak, desolate
moor.

Throughout the prince's wanderings, his troubles seem
to have been greatly augmented by the wetness of the
season; and now the rain fell in torrents, and the wind
blew cold and piercingly directly in their teeth. To add
to the wretchedness of their situation, there seemed no
possibility of procuring anything to eat; and about the
middle of the day the prince was so overcome by fatigue
and hunger, that he was almost unable to proceed. At
this juncture they happily came upon a small hut where
they begged for shelter and refreshment. On the inmates
being informed that they had fought at Culloden, and
that they were now fleeing from pursuit, they were
warmly received by the inmates and entertained with the
best which their poor means afforded. After resting, the
fugitives again set out for Rossinish, and towards evening
came as near to it as was safe to venture by daylight.
Here the prince, shivering with cold and wet, lay down
upon the high, open heather, there being no other shelter
from the pitiless storm. When night fairly set in, they
resumed their journey, but, the storm still continuing,
the wind and rain beat in their faces, and the darkness
was so complete that they could scarcely see a yard before
them. After numberless difficulties and misfortunes, they
at length drew near the hovel which had been fixed upon
as a place of meeting, and where they hoped to find Flora
Macdonald waiting for them. Mackechan went forward,
as a precaution, to see if the coast was clear; but instead
of finding the lady on whom their hopes depended, he
learned, to his consternation, that a company of the Skye
Militia had landed near, the day before, and had now

actually pitched their tents within a quarter of a mile of
the appointed rendezvous.   With this bad news, and
without any information of Flora Macdonald, Neil had to
return to the prince.   On hearing it, he seemed more
cast down than he had hitherto seemed to appear, no
matter what perils had surrounded him.   He ventured,
in spite of the near neighbourhood of his pursuers, to take
shelter in the hovel for two or three hours at night; but
he was forced to leave it at daybreak, as the soldiers
visited it for several mornings to procure milk; and all
the day he had to lie concealed in a small cave by the sea-
shore.

"It is almost impossible," says an account purporting to
be written by Mackechan himself, "to describe what
sufferings the prince endured under that miserable rock,
which had neither sufficient height nor breadth to cover
him from the rain, which poured in torrents; and to
aggravate his misfortunes, his face and hands were attacked
by swarms of midges, which caused him great pain.   Neil,
who was continually with him, did everything he could
to alleviate his sufferings, and in this miserable condition
the prince remained for some time, till a faithful dairymaid at length brought information that the prince might
return to the house, as the militia had now left the
district.   Neil now helped him to his feet, and they walked
together to the house, where the same dairymaid had prepared a comfortable room for their reception."

It is worthy of record that the dairymaid knew who
the royal fugitive was, and was also aware of the splendid
reward offered for his body dead or alive; but the mag-
nificent bribe offered for his betrayal was no temptation
to her.   She visited the prince in his concealment as often
as she could, and brought him food, together with information as to the movements of his enemies.

In the meantime, Flora Macdonald, for whom they looked so anxiously, was unavoidably detained by the difficulty of procuring the articles necessary for the execution of her plan, till the prince, not able longer to endure the suspense, and wishing at least to know the worst, despatched a messenger in search of her.

On the third day after his arrival at Rossinish, the prince's anxiety was relieved by the intelligence that Flora Macdonald, accompanied by Lady Clanronald, was approaching by sea. At this joyful information the prince forgot his danger, and, with his natural gallantry, hastened to the beach, where he offered his hand to Lady Clanronald, Captain O'Neil performing the same service to our heroine, and conducted them to the hut.

This was not the first meeting of Prince Charles and Lady Clanronald; she had before visited him, with her husband, under circumstances of equal wretchedness, and had been zealous to furnish him with everything within her power to assist him. In this case, the prince remembered the previous favours he had received, and did his best to entertain his benefactress. He personally assisted in preparing a homely dinner, which had been provided for himself, and, when all was ready, the party sat down to the table, Flora on the right hand of the prince, and Lady Clanronald on his left, and although every one present was fully alive to the exigencies of the case, and the peculiar strangeness of the circumstances, they partook of a hearty and welcome meal. When one of the company expressed their sorrow at the altered fortunes of the prince, and his present miserable condition, he replied with a smile:

"It would be well for all kings if they could pass through the ordeals of hardships and privations which it has been my lot to undergo."

While yet occupied at dinner, Lady Clanronald's servant came to break up the pleasant party with the alarming intelligence that General Campbell had landed in the neighbourhood with a large force; and soon after came the news that Captain Fergusson, with an advanced party, was within two miles of them, on his way to Lady Clanronald's house at Ormaclade. Under these circumstances it was necessary for that lady to hasten home, where she had afterwards to undergo a strict examination from the same Captain Fergusson, who, however, elicited nothing from her. Some time after, Lady Clanronald and her husband were arrested for the part they had acted in aiding the escape of the prince;—they were conveyed to London, where they remained a year in custody.

After the departure of Lady Clanronald, it was considered advisable that the prince should at once assume his female disguise. It consisted of a flowered linen gown, a light-coloured quilted petticoat, a white apron, and a mantle of dun camlet, made after the Irish fashion, with a hood. His disguise was completed, says an authority, "not without some mirth and raillery passing amidst all their distress and perplexity, and a mixture of tears and smiles."

On setting out, the prince bade farewell to his faithful companion, Captain O'Neil, who would gladly have accompanied them farther; but Miss Macdonald would not hear of this. With Neil Mackechan, therefore, for their guide, they proceeded a short distance along the coast to the place where a boat was waiting for them, which they reached extremely wet and fatigued. As it would be dangerous to embark before nightfall, they lighted a fire among the rocks, but they had scarcely begun to enjoy its warmth, before they were forced to extinguish it, on account of the approach of some small boats. Happily, however, these boats pulled past the spot where the fugitives were concealed without the slightest discovery being made.

On the 28th of June the unfortunate party embarked on board the small boat which had been provided for them. The weather was favourable at starting, but towards night a storm arose, and for a considerable time they were in great danger. Miss Macdonald herself betrayed some alarm at their perilous situation, and the boatmen even exhibited some uneasiness; but the spirits of Prince Charles did not flag, and to encourage and cheer his companions he told them cheerful stories, and lightened their labours with pleasant songs.

The storm died away as the morning approached, and towards daybreak they reached Waternish, on the western part of the Isle of Skye, which, being usually a deserted place, was thought a safe place for landing. To their dismay, however, it was found to be in the possession of the militia, who had three boats drawn up on the beach, each happily without oars. The fugitives, discovering the position of matters, at once pulled hastily from the shore. Being discovered by the guard they were ordered to return and surrender themselves, muskets were pointed at them, and even instructions to fire were threatened. At no point of the prince's wanderings had his situation been more critical; for not only was the boat's party threatened from the shore, but several royal cruisers were in sight, so as to make escape seem almost impossible. The boat, however, contained brave and noble hearts; and when at length the troops on the shore were ordered to fire, the bullets whistled over their heads, but the boatmen strained every nerve, urged on by the exhortations of the prince "not to fear the villains." The boatmen assured their royal passenger that they had no fear of themselves, but only for him, to which he replied, with great cheerfulness:

"Oh, there is no fear for me." The prince then urged
Flora to lie down in the bottom of the boat, as the safest
shelter from the bullets which were now flying round the
boat; but sustained by the cause which she was engaged
in, she showed no fear, and entreated him, whose life was
of so much more importance, to take the place of the
greatest security. He still urged her, but she refused
unless he would follow her example, which, with some
unwillingness, he was at length prevailed upon to do.

They shortly got out of reach of their enemies, and
proceeded on their voyage in a calm sea. Exhausted by
excitement and fatigue, Flora Macdonald fell fast asleep
at the bottom of the boat. Charles, who throughout
seems to have felt the most tender and grateful interest
in his young preserver, now devoted himself to protect
her slumbers, and, fearing that the boatmen might accidentally disturb or hurt her, sat by her side, watchful,
lest even an unguarded noise should awaken her.

After rowing for twelve miles, the party landed at
Kilbride, near Mugstat, the seat of Sir Alexander Macdonald, formerly an adherent to the cause of the prince,
but who had since deserted him. He was fortunately
absent at Fort Augustus on duty. Flora, as agreed upon,
left the prince on the beach while she proceeded to meet
Lady Margaret Macdonald, the loyal wife of the recreant
chieftain, to inform her of the landing of the royal fugitive,
and for which, of course, she must necessarily have been
unprepared. On arriving at the house, Flora found that
Captain Macleod, commandant of the militia quartered
near, was actually on a visit there—a circumstance extremely likely to disconcert her; but, with admirable
presence of mind, she entered into conversation with him,
and answered with the utmost composure the various
questions he put to her, keeping up the same unembar-

rassed deportment during dinner, and conversing with
him in a friendly and amiable manner. Another guest at
dinner was Alexander Macdonald, of Kingsburgh, a noble-
minded and devoted old man, and a warm adherent of the
exiled prince. Flora well knew him to be such, and finding some difficulty in communicating with the lady of the
house, she was glad to impart her important secret to
him, requesting him to inform Lady Margaret at the very
earliest moment, of the situation and position of the
prince. It might be some thought of her husband's different views which caused the poor lady to be so greatly
alarmed on hearing this news; for on Macdonald of Kingsburgh informing her where Charles was, she could not
command herself, but screamed with terror, and exclaimed,
that she and her family were ruined for ever. Yet those
were not unreasonable fears, for the indiscriminate cruelties
practised by the successful party since the battle of Culloden, had been such as to strike terror into the boldest
heart; and Lady Margaret might well dread the vengeance
of the conqueror on so daring an act as that of yielding
protection to the proscribed prince. Kingsburgh, however, succeeded in calming her.

"For his part," he said, "he was an old man, and was
quite willing to take the hunted prince into his own
house; he had but one life to lose, and it mattered little
to him whether he died with a halter round his neck, or
whether he awaited a natural death, which, in the common course of nature, could not be far distant."

After a long conference between Lady Margaret,
Kingsburgh, and Donald Roy, another warm adherent
of the prince, who was called into their confidence, it was
agreed that it would be best for the prince to accept the
offer of Kingsburgh, and to take shelter in his house at
Portree for the present, and from which he could cross over

to the island of Raasay.　This important matter was discussed in the garden, while Miss Macdonald entertained the lieutenant in the house.　Flora maintained her composure, though she was mentally fretted by Lady Margaret's restlessness in continually passing in and out of the room.　Mackechan was sent to inform the prince of what had been determined upon, and of Kingsburgh's approach. The latter, providing himself with a bottle of wine and some biscuits, set out in search of the prince, whom he had never yet seen.　He had some difficulty in finding him, but the sudden flight of a flock of sheep, as if they had been scared by the sight of a human being, guided him to the spot where he found the royal fugitive in his disguise, and grasping a great stick, his only weapon, as a defence, in case of surprise.　Having satisfied himself of the friendly intention of his visitant, Charles expressed himself ready to set out immediately on the route proposed for him; but first partook of the welcome refreshment which Kingsburgh had brought, and entered into familiar conversation with his new friend, in the course of which Kingsburgh happened to say that he had visited Mugstat that day by mere accident, and that he did not know his reason for doing so.

"I will tell you the cause," replied the prince; "Providence sent you there to take care of me."

Throughout his wanderings Prince Charles frequently thus expressed his sense of being under divine protection, and to this cause attributed his many wonderful escapes. Those who attended him through his wearying and harassing adventures, have recorded that he was always regular and serious in his devotions under the most adverse circumstances.　How sad that the conduct of later years should have obscured so fair a promise!

As soon as Flora Macdonald could depart without

exciting suspicion, she rose from the table and took a formal leave of her hostess; who, in her turn, affected to be extremely averse to part with her guest.

"When you were last here," said Lady Margaret reproachfully, "you promised next time you came to pay me a long visit."

Miss Macdonald, however, desired to be excused at that time, because she wanted to see her mother, and to be at home in these troublous times. After several civilities of this kind, Lady Margaret consented to her going; only assuring her that she would not allow her to pay so short a visit next time.

The prince being already on the way with Kingsburgh to his house, Flora, with Mackechan, Mrs. Macdonald of Kirbihost, and her two servants, set out on horseback on the same route, and presently overtook the disguised fugitive and his friend. The prince seemed to have failed entirely in assuming the feminine manner becoming the costume which he wore. Flora, in order to avert the suspicion which she feared would be raised by his strange appearance, urged her party to a brisk trot as they passed him; but even then the awkward gait of the prince did not escape the sharp eyes of one of the maids.

"I think," said the girl, "I never saw such an impudent-looking woman as Kingsburgh's walking with. I daresay she's either an Irishwoman or a man in woman's clothes; look what long stride she takes, and how awkwardly she manages her petticoats."

Miss Macdonald readily replied that she knew her to be an Irishwoman, for she had seen her before.

The riding party passed, and the prince went striding on, exciting the alarm of his guide by his awkwardness; at one time, in crossing a brook, he lifted his petticoats so high as to oblige Kingsburgh to expostulate on his rude-

ness, and in avoiding this extreme at the next ford he
suffered all his garments to float upon the water. Alarmed
for the consequences of sustaining his character so ill,
Kingsburgh thought it best to leave the public road, and
pursue their journey to his house across the hills. The
rain came on, and they were soon drenched to the skin.
When they reached the house it was twelve o'clock at
night, and Flora Macdonald, who had parted with her
companions and man-servant on the road, had arrived
there a short time before.

Kingsburgh led his illustrious guest into the hall, and
then sent up a servant to his wife, to inform her that he had
arrived with a party of guests, who stood much in need
of refreshment. The lady had retired to rest, and not
thinking it necessary to disturb herself, sent a message
to her husband and his guests, hoping they would make
themselves welcome with whatever they could find in the
house. As she spoke, her little girl, of seven years old,
who, strangely enough, seems to have been still out of
bed, ran into her mother's room to tell her, in great
alarm, that her father had brought home the "most odd,
muckle, ill-shaped wife she had ever seen, and had taken
her into the hall, too." Kingsburgh, on receiving his
wife's message, at once went to his wife's room, and in a
mysterious manner, urged her to rise and dress without
delay, and attend to the necessities of their guests.

Without suspecting the real truth, Lady Kingsburgh
at once guessed that her husband had brought with him
some person of distinction implicated in the late troubles.
She therefore hastened to obey his wishes; and while she
got herself ready, sent her little girl down to the hall for
her keys; but the child ran back more alarmed than
before, saying, she could not go for the keys, for the
muckle woman was walking up and down in the hall;

and she was afraid of her. Her mother was therefore obliged to fetch them herself, and went into the hall. The prince was seated at the end of the room when she entered; but, on seeing her he rose, and, probably supposing that she knew his secret, saluted her. Her surprise was completed on feeling the rough beard of a man against her cheek. Neither uttered a word, however; and she hastened to tell her husband that this pretended woman was some unfortunate gentleman escaped from Culloden, and inquired whether he had brought any tidings of Prince Charles. Her husband took both her hands in his and answered.

"My dear, it is the prince himself!"

"The prince," she cried in great terror; "then we are all ruined! We shall all be hanged now!"

"Never mind, wife," said he, "we can die but once; and if we are hanged for this, we shall die in a good cause." He then bade her get ready a supper of eggs, butter, and cheese, or whatever else was in the house.

"Eggs, butter, and cheese," she answered; "that is not a supper for a prince!"

"Wife," said her husband, "you little know how he has fared lately. Your supper will be a feast to him; besides, if we were to make it a formal meal, it would rouse the suspicions of the servants, and you must therefore make haste with what you can get, and come to supper yourself."

"*Me* come to supper!" exclaimed the good woman. "I couldna behave myself before royalty."

"But you must come," was the reply; "for the prince will not eat a bit without you; and he is so obliging and easy in conversation, that you will have no difficulty in behaving before him."

Thus urged, she consented, and had the pleasure of

sitting on one side of the prince, while Flora Macdonald
sat upon the other, and of seeing him do full justice to the
plentiful though homely meal she provided for him, before
he retired to rest.   The poor, hunted prince, as he afterwards said himself, had almost forgot what a bed was, and
in the enjoyment of so rare a luxury, the more delightful
from the fatigues he had undergone, he slept longer than
seemed safe to Miss Macdonald, who was naturally anxious
to be on their way.   Having waited impatiently till ten
in the morning, she urged her host to go and rouse him;
but when Kingsburgh entered the prince's room, he found
him in so sound a sleep, that he had not the heart to
wake him, and did not disturb him till one o'clock.

Though the female dress of the prince had been worn
with too little skill to be a safe disguise, and it had been
decided to give it up; yet, to avoid the suspicions of servants, it was thought necessary that he should resume it
for a short time.   He therefore dressed himself as on the
previous day, and summoned Lady Kingsburgh and Miss
Macdonald to put the finishing touches to his attire, and
to "dress his head."

Lady Kingsburgh, who had got over her first fears,
entered with spirit and feeling into the scene.   She afterwards, in speaking of it, told her friends that the prince
laughed heartily during the process, with the same glee
as if he had been trying on a girl's clothes for a frolic.

When Miss Macdonald was about to put on his cap,
Lady Kingsburgh spoke to her in Gaelic, to ask the
prince for a lock of his hair; but she declined doing so,
as if shrinking from what might seem too bold a request.
The prince, however, inquired what they were talking
about, and she then told him what Lady Kingsburgh had
asked her to do.   He immediately laid his head in her
lap, and told her to cut off as much as she pleased.   She

then cut off a lock which she divided between Lady Kingsburgh and herself. The prince also changed his worn-out shoes for a pair of new ones. The old ones, all the more precious from the hard services they had undergone, were long preserved as a relic by Kingsburgh, and after his death were cut up into small pieces, which were distributed among his Jacobite friends.

After taking a grateful leave of Lady Kingsburgh, the prince set forward on his journey to Portree, under the guidance of Flora Macdonald and his host, expecting to find a boat there to take him to Raasay. As soon as he was gone, Lady Kingsburgh hastened to the room which had been occupied by Prince Charles, and taking the sheets he had lain in from the bed, she folded them carefully up, and declared they should never again be used or washed during her life, but would serve her for a winding-sheet after she was dead. She afterwards, at Flora Macdonald's request, gave one of them to her, who carefully preserved it for the same purpose.

When it was considered safe to do so, Charles changed his disguise for a Highland dress, and then took an affectionate leave of his host, both shedding tears at the parting.

The prince, accompanied by Neil Mackechan, and with a boy for their guide, proceeded through by-ways to Portree; while Flora Macdonald went thither on horseback by another way, the better to gain intelligence, and at the same time to prevent discovery.

The clothes the prince had worn were hid in a bush, and afterwards removed by Kingsburgh to his own house; but it was thought safe to destroy everything that might tell against him in the event of a discovery. His daughter, however, begged that the gown might be spared, both as a record of the prince, and as being of a pretty

pattern. Thus rescued, a chronicler says that "a Jaco
bite manufacturer afterwards got a pattern made from it,
and sold an immense quantity of cloth precisely similar
in appearance to the loyal ladies of Scotland."

In the meanwhile, by their different roads, the prince
and Flora Macdonald approached Portree. Great exertions had been made by his adherents to have a suitable
boat there in readiness to carry him over to Raasay.
When all was waiting, with zealous friends and able
boatmen in attendance, Donald Roy repaired alone to
the only public-house in Portree, to receive any intelligence that might be brought him of the prince. Here he
was joined by Flora Macdonald, who informed him that
Charles was approaching; and within half an hour the
latter appeared, but wet through and in a miserable plight.
These annoyances, however, did not make him forget the
consideration due to the lady who had thus devoted herself to his service: he thought of her, while his faithful
friends thought only of his own comfort. He made himself as comfortable as circumstances would permit; but
when Donald Roy expressed his regret that he should
have had such adverse weather, he replied:

"I am more sorry that *our lady*"—for so he always
designated his fair protectress—"should have been exposed to such a night."

Having thus conducted the prince to Portree, Flora
Macdonald had completed her task, and done Charles all
the service it was in her power to render him. Next
morning, therefore, they took a final leave of each other.
He then bade her an affectionate farewell, and, saluting
her, said:

"For all that has happened, madame, I hope we shall
yet meet at St. James's."

Her visit to London, however, was to be made under

PRINCE CHARLES BIDS FAREWELL TO FLORA MACDONALD.

different auspices. Here, too, Charles took leave of his faithful attendant, Neil Mackechan, who was to return with Miss Macdonald to her mother's house at Armadale. He afterwards escaped safely to France, where he rejoined the prince.

After Flora had watched the boat containing the prince until it was out of sight she returned home, travelling for this purpose a fatiguing journey of many miles. With very remarkable caution she kept her late proceedings a profound secret, even from her mother. This precaution, however, afterwards seems to have been unavailing. The share which Flora Macdonald took in the escape of Prince Charles from Scotland transpired through some means; and she soon afterwards heard that Kingsburgh's house had been searched for her, and that the authorities were even acquainted with nearly every circumstance which occurred on her notable journey, and also with the fact that the prince had escaped in the disguise of a female.

A Captain Ferguson, who was conspicuous for his harshness, and even cruelty, to those who came under his charge at that time, was sent with a party of troops to search Kingsburgh's house, which he did in an insolent manner; but being met by Lady Kingsburgh, she gave him such answers, guarded on her part, and evidently acceptable or serviceable to him, that he proceeded farther in his search for the whereabouts of the prince.

After Flora had been at home for eight days she received a message from one of her own clan—Donald Macdonald, of Castleton, about four miles from her own house, to come to see him. He was a kinsman of Flora's family, and had been desired to arrange this meeting by the commanding officer of a company of troops stationed near at hand. Miss Macdonald was somewhat suspicious of this message, and in her perplexity she resolved to consult her friends as to what she ought to do. They were all strongly of opinion that she ought not to go—at least, not till next day—but, probably thinking that a refusal might prejudice her and create suspicion, she determined to obey the summons. On her way to the house of her kinsman she met an officer with a party of soldiers, who were coming to her mother's house in pursuit of her, and by them she was arrested.

On being examined she admitted, as previously agreed on with her friends, that she had given a passage in her boat to a tall, strong-looking woman, who represented herself as a soldier's wife, and whom she allowed to cross over with her to Skye—that this woman had left her, thanking her for the favour—but denied any knowledge of what had become of her. These answers were not considered satisfactory, and she was sent at once, a prisoner, on board ship, without being allowed leave to return home, or even to procure a change of apparel. The vessel was called the *Furnace*, and she was conveyed on board of it as a prisoner. To her extreme dismay she found that Captain Ferguson was commander of the vessel, or at all events he held the power of instructing the officer in charge of it. Fortunately, however, he did not come on board, and she was otherwise treated with consideration and unexpected respect. General Campbell, a gentleman of kindness and feeling, happened to be on deck when Flora came on board, and perhaps his influence had something to do with the treatment of the heroic prisoner. One of the lieutenants gave up his cabin for the accommodation of Flora and her maid; and three weeks afterwards, when the *Furnace* happened to be cruising in the neighbourhood of Armadale, she was allowed, under a slight escort, to go on shore to take leave of her friends, being specially enjoined, however, neither to converse in Gaelic, or speak out of hearing of those who had charge of her. After a stay of two hours on shore she returned on board ship.

Shortly afterwards Miss Macdonald was removed to the *Eltham*, commanded by Commodore Smith, who showed the utmost respect and regard for his prisoner. In this vessel Miss Macdonald met Captain O'Neil, the companion of her recent adventure, and her rejected suitor.

She immediately approached him, and playfully patting him on the cheek, said :

"To that black face I owe all my misfortunes."

He encouraged her, however, with the assurance that she need not be ashamed or afraid of the part she had taken in the escape of the prince. Indeed, there was something too certain of exciting general sympathy and admiration in a young and beautiful lady having thus devoted herself to the adventurer's cause, for those in power, however harsh in their general dealing, to venture on any strong act of severity towards her; nor does it seem to have been apprehended for her. The officers of the *Eltham* showed themselves extremely anxious to prove their private estimation of her conduct by allowing her every indulgence in their power.

Flora Macdonald was detained on board ship for five months, three months of which were passed in Leith Roads, close to the city of Edinburgh. While the vessel was in the "roads" the lady was an object of interest and curiosity to persons of all principles and opinions, and the well-wishers of the Stuart family were zealous in proving to her how thoroughly they appreciated her heroism, and the success of her efforts, while the ladies of the same party vied with each other in loading her with presents suited to her requirements, and everything which could possibly lessen the severities of her confinement.

The officers courteously permitted her to receive visits from her friends, and others who chose to call upon her, and the conversations which they had the pleasure to hold with her were of mutual gratification.

She narrated to some of them, that during the passage to the Isle of Skye a very heavy rain fell, which, with former fatigue, distressed her much. To divert her Prince Charles sang several pleasant songs. She afterwards fell asleep, and to keep her so the prince continued to sing. Happening to awake through some little bustle in the boat, she found the prince leaning over her, with his hands spread about her head. She asked what was the matter. The prince told her that one of the oarsmen, being obliged to do something with the sail, was compelled to step over her—the boat being so small—and lest he should have done her hurt, either by stumbling or trampling on her in the dark, he had done his best to preserve his guardian from harm. When Flora was telling this particular part of the adventure to some ladies who were paying their respects to her, one of them cried out with rapture:

"Oh, Miss Macdonald, what a happy creature you must be, to have had that dear prince to lull you asleep, and to take care of you, with his hands spread about your head when you were sleeping! You are surely the happiest woman in the world!"

"I could," said another lady, "wipe your shoes with pleasure, and think it an honour to do so, when I reflect that you had the honour to have the prince for your hand-maid: we all envy you greatly."

About this time a rumour reached Flora Macdonald that Prince Charles had been taken, and by it she was deeply affected. Gaining an opportunity of talking privately with one who had come to visit her, she said with tears in her eyes:

"Alas! I am afraid now that all I have done has been in vain—the prince, I hear, is now in the hands of his enemies."

They endeavoured to make her believe that the report was false, but she would not be comforted till it was positively ascertained to be so.

While the *Eltham* lay in Leith Roads, Flora was never allowed to go on shore, though in every other respect the officers and crew were civil, courteous, and respectful to the highest degree, and always gladly received any visitors who came to see her. Commander Smith behaved like a father to her, and ordered everything that could conduce to her comfort to be carefully attended to; and Captain Knowles, of the ship *Bridgewater*, behaved to her in the most polite and attentive manner.

When company came to visit her she was allowed by both of these officers to call for anything on board, and conduct affairs as if she were in her father's house; and the servants in attendance had orders to attend to all her instructions as if she were more an honoured guest than an unfortunate prisoner. Miss Macdonald was also allowed the privilege of inviting any guests she preferred to meet, to dine with her, and otherwise to exercise any liberty she pleased. Her behaviour in company was so easy, modest, and well-adjusted, that every visitor was surprised; for she had never been out of the islands of South Uist and Skye till about a year before the arrival of the prince, and previous to that she had only been, for ten or eleven months, on a visit to the family of Macdonald of Largoe, in Argyleshire.

"Some," says the personal narration which was after-

wards written, "that went on board to pay their respects
to her, used to take a dance in the cabin, and to press her
strongly to partake of that enjoyment in their company,
but with all their importunity they could not prevail upon
her to take a trip. She told them that at present her
dancing days were gone, and she would not readily entertain a thought of that diversion till she could be sure of
her prince's safety, and perhaps not till she could be
blessed with the happiness of seeing him again. Although
she was easy and cheerful, yet she had a certain mixture
of gravity in all her behaviour, which became her situation exceedingly well, and set her off to great advantage.

"She is of a low stature, fair complexion, and well
enough shaped. One would not discern by her conversation that she had spent all her former days in the High-
lands; for she talks English, or rather Scotch, easily, and
not at all with a Gaelic tone or accent. She has a sweet
voice and sings well; and no lady, Edinburgh bred, can
acquit herself better at the tea-table than she did in the
ship's cabin in Leith Roads. Her wise conduct in one of
the most perplexing scenes that can happen in life, her
fortitude and good sense, are memorable instances of the
strength of the female mind, even in those whose years
are tender and inexperienced."

In November, 1746, Miss Macdonald was conveyed to
London on board the *Bridgewater*, there to be placed at
the disposal of the government. Amid the general severities of the period she, however, had never any reason to
complain of harshness. Her captivity was rendered as
easy and comfortable as every circumstance would permit; and though under strict surveillance, she was allowed
to reside with a private family, where she had every
attention paid to her comfort.

This leniency has been attributed to the intercession of

the Prince of Wales, who had the generosity to admire an act of heroism, though performed against his private interest. When the Princess of Wales expressed herself in strong terms against the indulgence of government towards Flora Macdonald, he gave her a kind and yet a severe rebuke. "Madam," he said, "under similar circumstances would you not have done the same? I hope, I am sure you would."

When Miss Macdonald was ultimately set at liberty she was entertained with great distinction by the dowager Lady Primrose, in London—the same zealous lady who afterwards received Prince Charles on his first secret visit to London. Here she met with such universal and flattering attention as would have turned a less steady brain. But her natural simplicity and modesty preserved her in this new form of danger; and in the midst of so much to excite vanity and love of display her first wish seems to have been to return to her own quiet Highland home. Before being able to do so she was visited by persons of the highest rank; and when she left London she was presented with the sum of nearly fifteen hundred pounds by the Jacobite ladies of the metropolis.

Flora Macdonald returned to Skye in 1747, and three years afterwards was married to Alexander Macdonald of Kingsburgh, the younger son of the Macdonald who assisted her in the escape of Prince Charles; and thus she became closely connected with those who had shared the peril and honour of protecting the unfortunate Stuart in the time of his greatest trial.

Some years after her marriage, troubles, social and political, induced her and her husband and family to emigrate to America, where they purchased an estate in South Carolina. On the breaking out of the War of Independence, Kingsburgh, the husband of Flora, sided with the Royalists, and suffered imprisonment in consequence. On his release he took up arms against the Republicans; and when they gained the day he determined to return with his family to Scotland. On their passage home, however, they were attacked by a French ship. Before the action began all the women were ordered below, but Flora Macdonald, retaining her old spirit, refused to quit the deck, and by her words and example animated the courage of the sailors during a short but sharp engagement, which resulted in their favour. In the melée, however, Flora was thrown down and had her arm broken.

Ultimately her husband, herself, and family again settled in Skye, where she died in the seventieth year of her age, March 4, 1790. Her body was wrapped, according to her express desire, in the sheet which she had obtained from her mother-in-law on the eventful occasion of the visit of Prince Charles to her house. She was the mother of five sons, who all held commissions in the British army, and of two daughters, one of whom lived to an old age, inheriting her mother's features and principles.

DEBORAH SAMPSON,

THE HEROINE OF '76.

THERE are many incidents recorded in the history of the American Revolution in which acts have been achieved, and courage of the most daring character displayed, by females, which would have done honour to the stronger sex; but the narrative of life and character of the extraordinary woman whose story we are about to relate is without a parallel.

Like Jeanne d'Arc, we find a humble girl of seventeen inspired with an ardent patriotism and resolution to stand forth in the defence of her country; to aid in the struggle for freedom, or to perish, a noble sacrifice, in the attempt.

Deborah Sampson was born at Plympton, a small village in Massachusetts, on the 17th of December, 1760. When her parents were married her father was a respectable farmer; but through losses and misfortunes he became so impoverished as to be induced to undertake a seafaring life, and having made one voyage to Europe with tolerable success he started on a second, from which, alas! he never returned, his ship being wrecked, and himself and the greater part of his crew drowned.

The mother of Deborah, by her industry and economical management, kept her family together as long as she was able after the death of her husband; but sickness and other misfortunes compelled her to give the children into the hands of kind friends who had offered to take charge of them. Deborah was only five years old when she was adopted into the family of a lady named Fuller, who promised to take charge of her education.

She had not been more than three years in her new home when, to her great sorrow, her benefactress died. Her mother now removed her into the family of Mr. Jeremiah Thomas of the same town. Mrs. Thomas, perceiving in Deborah a great propensity for reading, writing, and study generally, gave her every opportunity to indulge it. She remained in that benevolent family till she attained her sixteenth year, when she was released from her indentures and became her own mistress. She then engaged herself to work in the family of a farmer one-half of her time, in payment for her board and lodging; the other half being spent at school. In a very few months she was regarded as a prodigy of learning, her proficiency being so rapid.

She was remarkable for her frequent interrogatories relating to natural history, especially the cultivation of plants, which became conspicuous in her early years, and was often heard to express her astonishment at finding any of her companions anxiously perusing a novel or romance founded on love stories. She frequently said that her mind was never more effectually impressed with the power, wisdom, and beneficence of God, than in the contemplation of his works.

The state of affairs in the colonies at this time began to wear a gloomy aspect, not only affecting the minds of men, but appearing most sensibly to interest the women also. Deborah Sampson never allowed a day to pass without anxiously inquiring what had last happened, and she seemed to follow the course of events with a sense of indignation against the opponents of American independence.

The distressed situation of the inhabitants of Massachusetts, and particularly those of Boston, can better be imagined than described. Deborah, though not an eye-witness of this distress, was not insensible to it; her mother and sisters were residing there, and she was continually hearing of the unprovoked insults of the inhabitants by the enemy, and the probability of their soon being in a starving condition. These startling relations filled her patriotic soul with an enthusiasm which strengthened and increased with the progress of the war, and fixed in her mind the accomplishment of the object after which she aspired. She had frequent opportunities of seeing the American volunteers as they marched from one post to another; every time she looked upon them added addi-tional stimulus to her determination; and the time had now arrived to carry into execution those plans which had long been maturing in her mind. During her resi-dence at the farm her master had permitted her to keep a few fowls, by which she had been able to save a small sum of money. She now determined that with this she would purchase some material which she could convert into male attire; and accordingly procured some fustian, and when secure from observation made it up into clothing suitable for her purpose. As each article was finished it was hid in some secure place, till the whole suit was complete.

She then made known to her employer that she was going where she would be better paid for her labour, and tying her new apparel into a bundle, left the house to enter upon a new, and, to her, a most hazardous enter-prise.

Early in the morning of her departure from the farm-house she rose before the sun, and retiring to the shelter of the nearest wood, assumed the garb in which she dared the most dangerous exploits. Deborah then took her course towards Taunton, hoping to meet with some one who was going directly to headquarters. She reached Taunton about six in the morning, and, unfortunately, the first person she met was a near neighbour of her late employer; he, however, failed to recognize her. She proceeded on to Bellingham, knowing that there was a recruiting party there, and when she arrived, offered to serve as a continental soldier during the war. The officer in charge gladly accepted such an admirable and serviceable recruit. She was entered as Robert Shurtliffe, and ordered to join the company of Captain Thayer, of the Uxbridge Regiment, at Worchester.

An authoress of the period relates an incident which occurred in Deborah's career at this time. She says: "The regiment not being ready to depart, and Captain Thayer being much pleased with the appearance of his new recruit, gave *him* a home in his family. While in the house of Captain Thayer, a young girl, visiting his wife, was much in the society of the young soldier. Coquettish by nature, and perhaps priding herself on the conquest of the young recruit, she suffered her growing partiality to be perceived. Robert, on his part, felt a curiosity to learn by new experience how soon a maiden's fancy might be won; and had no scruples in paying attentions to one so volatile and fond of flirtation, with whom it was not probable the impression would be lasting. This little piece of romance gave some uneasiness to the worthy Mrs. Thayer, who could not help observing that the liking of her fair visitor for Robert was not reciprocated. She took an opportunity of remonstrating with the young soldier, and showed what unhappiness might be the consequence of such folly, and how unworthy it was of a brave man to trifle with the affections of a girl. The caution was taken in good part, and it is not known whether the courtship was continued, though Robert received at parting some tokens of remembrance, which were treasured as relics in after years."

The company being ready, they were ordered to West Point, to be detached into their proper companies and regiments. It fell to the lot of Robert to be in Captain Webb's company of light infantry, in Colonel Sheppard's regiment, and in General Patterson's brigade. On the second day after their arrival they drew their accoutrements, which were a French fusee, a knapsack, a cartridge-box, and thirty cartridges. Her next business was to clean her piece, and to exercise every morning in the drill, and at four o'clock, p.m., on the grand parade. Her garb was exchanged for a uniform peculiar to the infantry of those times. It consisted of a blue coat, lined with white, and white wings on the shoulders, and cords on the arms and pockets; a white waistcoat, breeches or overalls and stockings, with black straps above the knees; half-boots, a black velvet stock, and a cap, with a variegated cockade on one side and a plume tipped with red on the other, and a white sash about the crown.

The martial accoutrements, exclusive of those in marches, were a gun and bayonet, and a cartridge-box with white belts. The company did not remain long at West Point before they received orders to join another part of the army then lying at Haarlem, near New York. As the infantry belonged to the rangers, a great part of their duty was that of scouting, which they followed in places most likely for success.

After remaining at Haarlem for a few days they were ordered to White Plains, where they, in turns, kept the lines; but nothing uncommon occurred in either of these two places.

Early in July Captain Webb's company, being on duty

in the morning, came up with a party of Dutch cavalry
from General Delancy's corps, then in Morrisiani. They
were armed with carbines and broadswords. The action
commenced on their side. The Americans stood two fires
before they got orders to retaliate. The ground was
warmly contested for a considerable time; at length the
infantry were obliged to give way till a reinforcement
arrived, when the enemy made a hasty retreat. Our fair
soldier said she suffered more from the intense heat of the
day than from the fear of being killed, although a soldier
at her left hand was shot dead, and three others wounded
very near her. She escaped with two shots through her
coat, and one through her cap.

During their stay at White Plains Generals Washington
and Rochambeau removed their main armies to the south-
ward; and orders were soon received that the part remaining near New York should immediately repair to
Williamsburgh, Virginia. They accordingly marched to
the city of New York, and embarked in ships to James-
town, where they landed and marched to Williamsburgh
and joined the main troops. On the morning after their
arrival General Washington reviewed the armies on
parade, when general orders were read to the soldiers;
after which Washington, placing himself immediately in
front of the ranks, said: "If the enemy should be tempted
to meet our army on its march the general particularly
enjoins the troops to place their principal reliance on the
bayonet, that they may prove the vanity of the boast
which the British make of their peculiar prowess in decid-
ing battles by that weapon."

Our young soldier happened to stand within ten yards
of General Washington when he made this remark, and
in after years she frequently said that he "spoke with
firm articulation and winning gestures; but his aspect

and solemn mode of utterance affectingly bespoke the great
weight that rested on his mind.

The soldiers were before mostly ignorant of the expedition upon which they were going, but from the information received by the affectionate addresses of their leaders
every countenance wore an agreeable aspect, and complete
harmony prevailed among them.   The phalanx composed
the advanced guards, and was commanded by the Marquis
Lafayette.   Our heroine was one of this company, and by
reason of the absence of a non-commissioned officer she
was appointed to supply his place.   After these prelimi-
naries had been adjusted they marched toward York-Town.
They came within two miles of it about sunset, when
Colonel Scammel, the officer of the day, brought word for
the armies to halt at that point, and that the soldiers
were to lie upon their arms all night.

Such orders, strange to say, seemed perfectly familiar
to our fair soldier; it did not excite in her even a terror,
although it was a prelude to imminent danger.

Anticipating no greater danger than she had before
experienced, although she foreboded a great event, she
acquiesced in the mandates of her officers with a calmness
that might have surprised an inexperienced soldier.   Next
morning, after the roll-call, they were reviewed, and went
through the quick motions of loading and firing blank-
cartridges, and exercise of the broadsword; and for more
than a week they were employed in throwing up their
works, sustaining frequent and heavy cannonading from the
besieged.   .

This came near proving too much for a female not yet
twenty years of age; but, being naturally ambitious, she
was unwilling to submit, although her hands were so
blistered that she could scarcely open or shut them.
Many apparently able-bodied men complained of their

inability to serve, and were relieved; this, instead of
being an example for her to follow, proved only an incentive to her exertions, and she determined to persevere as
long as nature would sustain her efforts.   On the ninth
day they completed their entrenchments, when a fierce
cannonade and bombardment commenced, which lasted all
night.   Next morning the French opened the redoubts
and batteries on the left, and a tremendous roar of cannons
and mortars continued all day.

Our heroine had never before seen the main armies
together; but now, brought into view of them, and led
on to a general engagement, she describes the ground as
actually trembling under her, from the tremendous firing
from both sides which had been kept up for a day and a
night.   She describes the night scenes as solemn and sublime to the highest degree, perpetual sheets of fire and
smoke belching forth as from a volcano, and towering to
the skies.   Two redoubts of the enemy having advanced
two hundred yards on the left, which checked the progress
of the American forces, it was proposed to reduce them
by storm.   For this purpose a select corps was chosen,
and the command given to Lafayette, with instructions
to act as he considered best.   Deborah was one of those
who marched to the assault with unloaded arms, but with
fixed bayonets.   The Americans soon obtained possession
of the redoubts, completely vanquishing the enemy.   As
they were leaving one of the forts a soldier clapped our
heroine on the back and said, "My lad, you are somewhat disfigured behind."   Not knowing what he meant,
she took no notice of the remark till an opportunity
presented, when she found the left skirt of her coat
hanging by a string, evidently having been cut with a
broadsword or a very close shot.   Matters now appeared
to be coming to a crisis, and nothing less than ruin or

an entire surrender awaited the British commander; he, however, capitulated on the 19th of October.

Our young soldier was within sight when the English general presented his sword to Washington; and in her relation of the scene she often remarked the magnanimity which he displayed through the whole of this trying scene. His country was saved! Thus was the grand pillar of war shattered to its base, and an ample foundation laid for the establishment of peace secured to a free people.

After a long and tedious march to the head of the Elk river, as well as a disagreeable voyage by sea, we find our heroine in her old quarters at West Point. On the arrival of the troops a colonnade was ordered to be commenced, on which she worked as hard as the most robust and expert soldier till the whole was finished. As soon as she found more leisure she determined on writing to her mother, for at times she felt unhappy at the distress her long absence, or supposed death, must have caused her. The letter she wrote was as follows:—

"DEAR PARENT,—On the margin of one of those rivers which intersects and winds itself so beautifully majestic through a vast extent of country of the United States is the present situation of your unworthy, but constant and affectionate daughter. I pretend not to justify, or even palliate my clandestine elopement.

"In hopes of pacifying your mind, which I am sure must be afflicted beyond measure, I write you this scrawl. I am in a large but well-regulated family. My employment is agreeable, although it is somewhat different and more intense than it was at home; but I apprehend it is equally advantageous.

"I have become mistress of many useful lessons, though I have many more to learn. Be not troubled, there-

fore, about my present or future engagements, as I will
endeavour to make that prudence my model for which,
I own, I am indebted to those who took charge of my
youth. Heaven grant that a speedy and lasting peace
may constitute us a happy and independent nation; that
I may once more return to the embraces of a parent
whom I love. Your affectionate daughter,

"DEBORAH SAMPSON."

"May, 1782."

A perusal of the foregoing letter will prove that
Deborah Sampson was not without a mind superior to
many she was obliged to make her associates; and that
morality and virtue were the talismans by which she was
to surmount the greatest difficulties. The business of war
at all times is nothing less than devastation, rapine, and
murder; and in the war of the American Revolution
these principles were never better exemplified. Hence
the necessity of scouting, which was the common business
of infantry, to which Deborah Sampson belonged.

A request was made by two sergeants and herself for
leave of their captain to retaliate on some refugees for
their outrageous insults to the inhabitants beyond their
lines. He replied: "You three dogs have contrived a
plan this night to be killed, and I have no men to lose."
He, however, reluctantly consented, and they beat for
volunteers. Nearly all the company turned out, but
only twenty were permitted to go; near the close of the
day they commenced their expedition. They passed a
number of guards, and went as far as East Chester undis-
covered, where they hid themselves in order to watch the
motions of those who might be on the plundering business. They quickly discovered that two parties had gone
out; and whilst they were contriving how to entrap

them they watched two boys who had been sent for
provisions to a private cellar prepared in the wood. One
of them informed them that a party had just been at his
mother's, and were gone to visit the Yankees who were
guarding the lines.   Concealing from them the fact that
they were Americans, they accompanied the boys to the
cellar or cave, which they found well stored with provisions of every description, and of which they made
good use.

Dividing into two parties of ten each, they sent out
sentinels, and again ambushed in a place called in Dutch,
Vonhoite.   About four o'clock on the following morning
they had a sharp skirmish with some of their opponents;
shots were rapidly exchanged, but on getting sufficiently
near they found their enemies had fled, actually leaving
their horses behind them.

Our heroine mounted an excellent horse, and with her
party pursued the runaways to the edge of a swamp,
where the latter begged for quarter, which was given to
them, and they were allowed to depart.   They soon came
up with another party, about thirty in number, who
seemed inclined to give them some more trouble.   Shots
were exchanged for a few minutes, when one of her party
was wounded, which made it necessary to retreat; at this
moment the dauntless young soldier felt a severe blow
just above her knee, and exclaimed to her comrades that
she was wounded, but not to any serious extent; but at
the same instant she felt something unusually warm
trickling down her neck, and putting her hand to the
place, found blood gushing from the left side of her head.
She said nothing, as she thought it no time to talk of
wounds unless mortal.   Her boots meantime were filled
with blood.

She told one of the sergeants that she was now so

seriously wounded she could ride no farther, and begged they would leave her just where she was. To this her comrades would not listen, and she was placed before one of them on a horse. A thousand thoughts at once darted through her mind, as she had always thought that she would rather die than that her sex should be disclosed to the army.

They at length, after riding in this painful manner for six miles, came to the French encampment, near what was called *Cron Pond*. Deborah afterwards said this ride was to her as if she was being carried to a place of execution. They were conducted by an officer of the guards to an old building, at that time used as an hospital, in which were a number of invalids, whose very appearance made her blood chill in her veins. The French surgeon came and prepared to dress her head. She said nothing of the other wound she had received; she requested the favour of more medicine than was necessary for her head; and taking an opportunity, with a penknife and a needle she extracted the ball from her knee, using afterwards the extra medicine she had obtained. She remained here for three weeks, and by attention both wounds were completely healed, one of them without the knowledge of any one but herself.

In the spring of 1783 peace began to be the general topic, and was at length announced in Congress. In April, General Patterson selected Robert Shurtliffe, otherwise Deborah Sampson, as his attendant, having previously become acquainted with his, or rather her, heroism and fidelity; and on the 19th of the same month cessation from hostilities was proclaimed, and the honorary badge of distinction, as established by Washington, conferred on the brave soldiers, of which our heroine was one of the recipients. The general became daily more attached to his new attendant, whom he treated more as an equal than as a subordinate; her martial deportment, added to her youthful and attractive appearance, filled him with admiration. With a detachment of 1500 men he was ordered to Philadelphia for the suppression of a mutiny among the American soldiers. Having some affairs of her general to arrange, Deborah did not go till four days afterwards, when she rode, in company with four gentlemen, through the Jerseys and part of Pennsylvania. In passing through one of the villages in Jersey, at the hotel where they were to remain for the night there happened to be a ball; the young soldiers were invited to join the party, where the youthful appearance and good manners of our heroine made her a prominent person for the evening. Little did she think that her winning manners would that night make a tender impression on one present, who would subsequently reveal to her the emotions she felt on her account.

They were detained at this place two days by an untoward circumstance which led to a duel between two officers, one of whom was killed.

On arriving at Philadelphia Deborah found the troops encamped on an eminence about half a mile from the city, where they had been placed on account of an epidemic which was raging there. Before many days had passed she fell a victim to the pestilence, and had to be removed to the hospital. In this place death itself could not have presented a more gloomy aspect; and to her it seemed not far distant, as multitudes were daily carried from it to their last home. She was placed in a room with two young officers of the same line, both of whom soon died, and she was left alone to ponder over her sad condition. Her disease seemed increasing, and at last she became so low that her attendant, believing that she was dead, had summoned the sexton to perform the last office. At this

moment one of the nurses coming in, wetted her lips
with cold water, which once more rallied the small remains of vitality and she showed signs of life.　During
the time that efforts were made to restore her the physician
was surprised to discover that Robert Shurtliffe was a
woman!　He had her immediately removed into the
matron's apartment, and from that time to her recovery
treated her with all the care that experience could bestow.
The thoughtful physician had the prudence to conceal this
important discovery from all but the matron; the latter,
on her part, also faithfully kept the secret.

Deborah slowly recovered, and became a welcome guest
in many wealthy families, still known only, however, as
a soldier.　We must here digress for a moment to relate
an incident without which this sketch would be bereft of
one of its most attractive features.

During their stay in the village in Jersey, and attendance at the ball before mentioned, our heroine became
acquainted with a young lady from Baltimore, who was
on a visit in that place.　This lady was the daughter of
a gentleman of wealth, and possessed considerable fortune
in her own hands.　At the ball our fair soldier was her
partner in the dance, and it so happened that they met
several times during the stay of the soldiers.　At first
the young lady attempted to check the impulse as the effect
of a giddy passion, but at length suffered it to play about
her heart unchided.

She followed the gallant young soldier to Philadelphia,
and hearing he was then in the hospital, she despatched
a messenger with a basket containing some choice fruit,
and the following letter:—

"DEAR SIR,—Fraught with the feelings of a friend
who is, doubtless beyond your conception, interested in

your health and happiness, I take the liberty to address you with a frankness which nothing but the purest friendship and affection can palliate. Know, then, that the charms I first read in your countenance brought a passion into my bosom for which I could not account. If it is from the thing called Love, I was before most strangely ignorant of it, and strove to stifle the fugitive, though I confess the indulgence was agreeable. But repeated interviews with you kindled it into a flame, I do not blush to own; and should it meet a generous return I shall not reproach myself for its indulgence. I have long sought to hear your residence; and how painful is the news I have this moment received that you are sick, if alive, in the hospital !

"Your complicated nerves will not admit of writing; but inform the bearer if you are in want of anything that money can purchase to conduce to your comfort; if you recover, and think proper to inquire my name, I will give you an opportunity; but if death is to terminate your existence, then let your last senses be impressed with the reflection that you die not without one more friend, whose tears will bedew your funeral obsequies. Adieu."

Some have been surprised, others charmed, by love from an unsuspected source, but our heroine alone can describe the effect and perturbation such a declaration had on her mind. She humbly returned her gratitude, at the same time saying she was not at that moment in want of anything with the exception of health.

In the evening she received a second basket of fruit, a bouquet of fragrant flowers, and a couple of guineas; the like favours being frequently repeated during her illness. But she knew not in whose bosom this flame was glowing, or whose heart contained so much worth.

Her health being now nearly restored, she was at times exceedingly distressed, fearing that a discovery had been made during her sickness.   Every zephyr became an ill-fated omen, and every salutation a mandate to summon her to a retribution for her assumption on the male character.   The physician, who had been so tender and kind to her during her illness, was now waiting a convenient opportunity to divulge to her his suspicion of her sex. He often found her dejected, and as he guessed the cause, introduced lively conversation. .He took an opportunity to introduce her to his daughters, who were very much pleased at the attentions and gallantry of so handsome a young soldier, little suspecting that their gallant, on the strength of whose arm and sword they had depended, was a female.

After she had prepared to join the troops, the doctor, availing himself of a private conference, asked her if she had any particular confidant in the army?   She replied, "Not one!" and, trembling, would have disclosed her secret; but seeing her confusion, he waived the question. Shortly afterwards General Patterson and two other officers, having occasion to visit Baltimore, took her with them.

On the next day after her arrival she received a note requesting her company for a few moments at a certain place.   Though confident she had before seen the writing, she could not conjecture from whom it came.   Prompted by curiosity, she went to the house as directed by the note, and being conducted into an elegant drawing-room was struck with admiration on finding alone a beautiful young lady of about seventeen years of age.   After the usual compliments on both sides the young lady very frankly but delicately confessed herself the author of the anonymous letter, and rehearsed her sentiments with an

unreservedness which evinced the sincerity of her passion
and the elevation of her soul.

This confession was the strongest evidence of the truth
of all that the young lady had declared; her effusions
flowed with affability, prudence, and dignified grace
which might have fired the breast of an anchorite. Deborah remained in this school of philosophy for two days,
promising to visit her young friend frequently. General
Patterson and his brother officers, having some business
with General Washington, proposed making a hasty visit
to Mount Vernon. Our heroine begged that she might
accompany them, for she needed time for reflection on
which way to act in this, to her, most trying affair, and
next, as she used to say, to take the last look at the
illustrious chief whom she so ardently loved and so delighted to serve. Having returned to Baltimore she,
according to promise, paid a visit to her attached friend,
feeling, as she thought, sufficient resolution to divest herself of the mask, or try in some way to divert a passion
which she feared had too much involved the happiness of
one of the choicest of her sex. After thanking her for
her generous esteem, and making many evasive apologies,
she represented that she was but a stripling soldier; and
that, had she inclination, indigence would forbid her settling
in the world. The innocent girl replied that sooner than
a concession should take place with reluctance, she would
forfeit the happiness which she could only find in the love
of the young soldier. But, she added, if want of interest
was the only obstacle, she was soon to be possessed of an
ample fortune in her own right. Touched with such a
pathetic union of love and beauty our fair soldier was
thrown off her guard, and her feelings found vent in a
flood of tears. She told the lady she must go to the north
to arrange some affairs and apply for her discharge, and in

a few months would return, when, if sne could conduce to her happiness, she would be supremely delighted. Thus parted the two lovers.

Immediately after their separation the young lady sent a messenger after our heroine with a present of twenty-five guineas, six linen shirts, and a watch, which is still in the possession of the descendants of this extraordinary female. The officers with their attendant, Robert, had arrived in Philadelphia; the following day General Patterson sent for our young soldier to his apartment. He was alone, and calling her to him, thus gracefully addressed her:

"Since you have continued nearly three years in the service of your country, always vigilant and faithful, and in many respects have distinguished yourself from your fellows, I would only ask, Does that martial attire which now glitters on your body conceal a female's form?"

Deborah was overwhelmed by the interrogatory, and fell on her knees before him; the good man raised her up, and pressing her to his bosom, presented her with a letter, saying:

"Here is your discharge, obtained the other day at Mount Vernon from our beloved father, the illustrious Washington; and here is a sum of money to defray your expenses to your family; your unrivalled achievements deserve ample compensation. Return to your friends, and assume that garb which you laid aside to aid in the struggles of your country."

Thus ended the military life of Deborah Sampson, the American soldier of 'seventy-six.

Her mother being still living, she returned to her home as an asylum from the calumny which necessarily would follow such a singular life, and to assume a course of duty which only could be an ornament to her sex. Shortly after her return home she commenced to keep a school, which she continued for four years, when she married Benjamin Gannett, a respectable farmer of Sharon, Massachusetts. They had three children, and Deborah lived to a great age; her husband, who outlived her, obtained a pension during the remainder of his life, by an act of Congress, entitled, "An act granting half-pay to widows or orphans, where their husbands or fathers served in the war of the Revolution."

During the presidency of General Washington, Deborah received a letter inviting Robert Shurtliffe, otherwise Mrs. Gannett, to visit Washington, and during her stay there Congress passed a bill granting her a pension and certain lands as a bounty for her services as a soldier in the war of the Revolution.

₊ The facts in the foregoing narrative have been compiled from Congressional documents, and information derived from the descendants of the illustrious soldier, therefore they may be relied upon as thoroughly authentic.

THE MAID OF SARAGOSSA.

SPAIN can boast of having produced heroines from the earliest records of history. The glorious memory of the women of Saguntum and Numantia, in the time of the Romans, and of Maria Pacheco, widow of the celebrated Padillo, may be paralleled in our days by the fame of Agustina, the Maid of Saragossa.

This illustrious maiden exposed her life for her king and country at the memorable siege of Saragossa, in 1808. General Le Fevre had been despatched by France in the June of that year to reduce Saragossa, the citizens of that town having bravely, but as the French thought contemptously, unfurled the royal standard of the Bourbons. Saragossa was not a fortified city: it was surrounded by an ill-constructed wall, twelve feet high by three broad, intersected by houses; these houses, the neighbouring churches and convents, were in so dilapidated a state, that in each of them from the roof to the foundation were to be seen immense breaches;—apertures begun by time and increased by neglect. A large hill, called Il Torero, commanded the town at a distance of a mile, and offered a situation for most destructive bombardment. Among the sixty thousand inhabitants there were but two hundred and twenty regular troops, and the artillery consisted of ten old cannons.

The French undervalued their foe, and began the siege in a very indifferent, almost slothful, manner. It was unnecessary, they thought, to use any great exertion, it being their impression that the only occupants of Saragossa were "monks and cowards." But their opinions and their efforts were destined to an entire revolution. Very seldom in the annals of war has greater heroism, greater bravery, greater horror and misery, been concentrated than during the two months that these desperate patriots repelled their invaders. No sacrifices were too costly to be offered, no extremities too oppressive to be endured by the besieged; but it often occurs that among the noblest bodies of men one sordid wretch may be found open to the far-reaching hand of corruption:—and such a wretch happened to be intrusted with the charge of a powder-magazine at Saragossa. Under the influence of French gold he fired the magazine on the night of the 2nd of June. To describe the horrors that ensued would be impossible. The French, to whom the noise of the explosion had been a signal, advanced their troops to the gates. The population, shrieking, shocked, and amazed, hardly knowing what had occurred, entirely ignorant of the cause, bewildered by conflagration, ruins, and the noise of the enemy's artillery unexpectedly thundering in their ears, were paralysed and powerless. The overthow, the slaughter of those who stood at the ramparts, seemed more like a massacre than a battle; in a short time the trenches presented nothing but a heap of dead bodies. There was no longer a combatant to be seen; nobody felt the courage to stand to the defence.

At this desperate moment an unknown maiden issued from the church of Nostra Donna del Pillas, habited in white raiment, a cross suspended from her neck, her dark hair dishevelled, and her eyes sparkling with supernatural lustre! She traversed the city with a bold and firm step; she passed to the ramparts, to the very spot where the enemy was pouring on to the assault; she mounted to the breach, seized a lighted match from the hands of a

dying engineer, and fired the piece of artillery which he
had failed to manage; then kissing her cross, she cried,
with the accent of inspiration:

"Death or victory!" and reloaded the cannon. Such
a cry, such a vision, could not fail to call forth enthusiasm;
it seemed as if aid in a just cause had been opportunely
sent from heaven; her cry was answered, "Long live
Agustina!"

"Forward, forward, we will conquer!" resounded on
every side. Nerved by such emotions, the power of every
man was doubled, and the French were repulsed on all
sides.

General Le Fevre, mortified at this unexpected result,
determined to reduce the place by starvation, and also to
distress it by bombardment from Il Torero. The pains
and sufferings that followed his measures are too horrible
to be detailed; but they afforded Agustina an opportunity
of displaying her intrepidity. She underwent frequent
perils in the endeavour to rescue unfortunate beings
wounded by the guns of the enemy, by the falling of
houses, timbers, or other casualties which, alas! befall all
places in a state of siege, and indeed all places where
war plays its dreadful havoc. Agustina went from
house to house, visiting the wounded, attending to their
injuries, or supplying aid to the sick and starving. The
French, by their indomitable perseverance, had, from
step to step, rendered themselves masters of nearly half
the city. Le Fevre thought his hour of triumph had
now certainly arrived—he demanded a capitulation from
Palafox, the commandant of Saragossa. Palafox received
it in public; he turned to Agustina, who stood near him
completely armed, and inquired, "What shall I answer?"

In a moment the patriot girl exclaimed, "War to the
knife!"

Her reply was echoed by the populace, and Palafox made her words his answer to Le Fevre.

Nothing in the history of war has ever been recorded to resemble the consequence of this refusal to capitulate. One row of houses in the street would be occupied by the Spanish, the opposite row by the French. A continual tempest of balls passed through the air; the town was a volcano; the most revolting butchery was carried on for eleven days and eleven nights. Every street, every house, was disputed with musket and poignard. Agustina ran from rank to rank, everywhere taking the most active part. The French were gradually driven back; and the dawn of the 17th of August saw them relinquish this long-disputed prey and take the road to Pampeluna. The triumph of the patriots, their joy, was unspeakable. Palafox rendered due honours to the brave men who had perished, and endeavoured to remunerate the few intrepid warriors who survived. Among them was Agustina. But what could be offered commensurate with the services of one who had saved the city? Palafox told her to select what honours she pleased—anything would be granted her. She modestly answered that she begged to be allowed to hold the rank of engineer, and to have the privilege of wearing the arms of the town of Saragossa. The rest of her life was spent in honourable poverty, until the year 1826, when she died,

"By all her country's wishes blest!"

Lord Byron in his *Childe Harold's Pilgrimage* thus makes mention of the circumstance which called forth the noble courage and daring of Agustina; and in the note which is attached to the original edition of the poem the facts on which the lines are based are stated.

(108)   L

"Is it for this the Spanish maid, aroused,
  Hangs on the willow her unstrung guitar,
  And, all unsex'd, the anlace hath espoused,
  Sung the loud song, and dared the deed of war?
  And she, whom once the semblance of a scar
  Appall'd, an owlet's larum chill'd with dread,
  Now views the column-scattering bay'net jar,
  The falchion flash, and o'er the yet warm dead
Stalks with Minerva's step where Mars might fear to tread.

"Ye who shall marvel when you hear her tale,
  Oh! had you known her in her softer hour,
  Mark'd her black eye that mocks her coal-black veil,
  Heard her light, lively tones in Lady's bower,
  Seen her long locks that foil the painter's power,
  Her fairy form, with more than female grace,
  Scarce would you deem that Saragoza's tower
  Beheld her smile in Danger's Gorgon face,
Thin the closed ranks, and lead in Glory's fearful chase.

"Her lover sinks—she sheds no ill-timed tear;
  Her chief is slain—she fills his fatal post;
  Her fellows flee—she checks their base career;
  The foe retires—she heads the sallying host:
  Who can appease like her a lover's ghost?
  Who can avenge so well a leader's fall?
  What maid retrieve when man's flush'd hope is lost?
  Who hang so fiercely on the flying Gaul,
Foil'd by a woman's hand, before a batter'd wall?"

NOTE.—Such were the exploits of the Maid of Saragoza,
who by her valour elevated herself to the highest rank of
heroines.   When the author (Lord Byron) was at Seville,
she walked daily on the Prado, decorated with medals
and orders, by command of the Junta.

The exploits of Agustina, the famous heroine of both
the sieges of Saragossa, are recorded in Napier's *History
of the Peninsular War*.   At the time when she first
attracted notice, by mounting a battery where her lover
had fallen, and working a gun in his place, she was in her

twenty-second year, exceedingly pretty, and in a soft feminine style of beauty. She had further had the honour to have her portrait painted by Sir David Wilkie, and also to be alluded to in Wordsworth's *Dissertation on the Convention of Cintra.* In a noble passage the poet concludes with these words:

"Saragossa has exemplified a melancholy, yea, a dismal truth,—yet consolatory and full of joy,—that when a people are called suddenly to fight for their liberty, and are sorely pressed upon, their best field of battle is the floors upon which their children have played; the chambers where the family of each man has slept; upon or under the roofs by which they have been sheltered; in the gardens of their recreation; in the street, or in the market-place; before the altars of their temples, and among their congregated dwellings, blazing or uprooted."

HELEN WALKER.

HELEN WALKER, the prototype of the immortal Jeanie Deans in Sir Walter Scott's novel *The Heart of Midlothian*, was a simple Scottish maiden, who saved her sister from a shameful and undeserved death. In doing so she voluntarily encountered untold difficulties and dangers rather than utter an untruth, by which she would readily and without further trouble have gained the same end.

In the following narrative we purpose giving only the facts in the life of the actual heroine as they occurred; but in order to show the graphic power with which the "Great Magician" displayed bare facts in the glowing hues of fiction, we would recommend all readers of the present sketch to peruse the *Chronicle of the Canongate* above referred to.

Helen Walker was the daughter of a small farmer in Dalwhairn, in the parish of Irongray, Dumfriesshire, where, after the death of her father, she continued to reside for some time as the support of her widowed mother, which she did by her own unremitting labour and while enduring many privations. On the death of her mother, Helen was left in charge of her sister, Isabella (who figures in the novel as Effie, or Euphemia Deans), who was much younger than herself, and whom she educated and maintained by severe personal exertions. Attached to her sister by natural and many other ties, it is not easy to conceive the feelings of Helen when she discovered that Isabella was about to be tried for the crime of child-murder, and that she herself was called upon to give evidence against her. In this moment of shame and anguish she was told by her sister's legal adviser, that if she could declare that her sister had made any preparations, however slight, or had given her any information on the subject, that such a statement would save the life of Isabella, as she (Helen) was the principal witness against her. To this remark the truthful and steadfast eldest sister replied:

"It is impossible for me to swear to a falsehood, whatever may be the consequence; I will give my testimony according to my conscience, and tell the truth, but nothing but the truth."

The trial came on, and Isabella Walker was found guilty and condemned to death. As she was removed from the bar she was heard to say to her sister: "Oh, Nelly, you have been the cause o' my death!" Helen replied: "Tibby, ye ken I bade to speak the truth."

In Scotland, at that time, six weeks had to elapse from the passing of judgment and the carrying out of the sentence; and of this precious interval Helen had thoroughly made up her mind to avail herself. Whether her scheme had been long and carefully considered, or was the inspiration of a bold and vigorous mind in the moment of its greatest anguish at her sister's reproach, we cannot tell; but on the very day of the condemnation she found strength for exertion and action. Her first step was to get a petition drawn up, in which was stated the peculiar circumstances of her sister's case; she then procured, through the assistance of friends, a sum of money necessary for her expenses, and that very same night set out on her journey, actually barefooted and alone, and in due time reached London in safety, having performed the whole

distance from Dumfries (a distance of nearly two hundred
and ninety miles) on foot. On her arrival in London
she immediately made her way to the residence of John,
Duke of Argyle. Without introduction or recommen-
dation of any kind, but simply wrapped in her tartan
plaid, and carrying her petition in her hand, she succeeded in gaining an audience, and presented herself
before the duke. She was afterwards heard to say that
by the strength which the Almighty gave her, she had
been able to meet the duke at a most critical moment,
which, if lost, would have taken away the only chance
of saving her sister's life. There must have been a most
convincing air of truth and sincerity about her, for the
duke interested himself at once in her cause, and immediately procured the pardon she so eloquently and affection-
ately petitioned for, with which she was able to return
on foot to Dumfries, just in time to save her sister's
life.

Isabella, or Tibby Walker, thus saved, as it were, from
the grave, was eventually married to the father of her
child, and lived for many years afterwards in the neighbourhood of Whitehaven, uniformly acknowledging the
extraordinary affection to which she owed her preservation.

Sir Walter Scott became acquainted with the remarkable episode in the life of Helen Walker through a communication which he received from Mrs. Goldie, wife of
Thomas Goldie, Esq., of Craigmuie, Commissary of Dumfries. Her communication was in these words :—

"I had taken for summer lodgings a cottage near the
old abbey of Lincluden. It had formerly been inhabited
by a lady who had pleasure in embellishing cottages,
which she found perhaps homely and even poor enough ;
mine, therefore, possessed many marks of taste and

elegance unusual in this class of habitations in Scotland, where a cottage is literally what its name declares.

"From my cottage door I had a partial view of the abbey. Some of the highest arches were seen over and some through the trees scattered along a lane which led down to the ruin, and the strange fantastic shapes of almost all those old ashes accorded wonderfully well with the building they at once shaded and ornamented.

"The abbey itself from my door was almost on a level with the cottage; but on coming to the end of the lane it was discovered to be situated on a high perpendicular bank, at the foot of which run the clear waters of the Cluden, where they hasten to join the sweeping Nith,

'Whose distant roaring swells and fa's.'

As my kitchen and parlour were not very far distant I one day went in to purchase some chickens from a person I heard offering them for sale. It was a little, rather stout-looking woman, who seemed to be between seventy and eighty years of age; she was almost covered with a tartan plaid, and her cap had over it a black silk hood, tied under the chin. Her eyes were dark, and remarkably lively and intelligent. I entered into conversation with her, and began by asking her how she maintained herself, &c.

"She said that in winter she footed stockings, that is, knit feet to country-people's stockings, which bears about the same relation to stocking-knitting that cobbling does to shoemaking, and is of course both less profitable and less dignified; she likewise taught a few children to read, and in summer she whiles reared a few chickens.

"I said I could venture to guess from her face she had never been married. She laughed heartily at this, and said:

"'I maun hae the queerest face that ever was seen, that ye could guess that. Now, do tell me, madam, how cam ye to think sae?'

"I told her it was from her cheerful disengaged countenance. She said, 'Mem, have ye na far mair reason to be happy than me, wi' a gude husband and a fine family o' bairns, and plenty o' everything. For me, I'm the puirest o' a' puir bodies, and can hardly contrive to keep myself alive in a' the wee bits o' ways I hae tell't ye!'

"After some more conversation, during which I was more and more pleased with the old woman's conversation and the *naïveté* of her remarks, she rose to go away, when I asked her name. Her countenance suddenly clouded, and she said gravely, rather colouring: 'My name is Helen Walker; but your husband kens weel about me.'

"In the evening I related to my husband how much I had been pleased, and inquired what was extraordinary in the history of the poor woman. He replied: 'There were perhaps few more remarkable people than Helen Walker;' and he repeated the story as it has been already stated.

"I was," continues Mrs. Goldie in her communication to Sir Walter Scott, "so strongly interested by this narrative that I determined immediately to prosecute my acquaintance with Helen Walker; but as I was to leave the country next day I was obliged to defer it till my return in spring, when the first walk I took was to Helen Walker's cottage.

"She had died a short time before. My regret was extreme, and I endeavoured to obtain some account of Helen from an old woman who inhabited the other end of her cottage. I inquired if Helen ever spoke of her past history, her journey to London, &c. 'Na,' the old woman said, 'Helen was a wily body, and whene'er ony o' the neebors asked onything about it, she aye turned the conversation.'

" In short, every answer I received only tended to increase my regret, and raise my opinion of Helen Walker, who could unite so much prudence with so much heroic virtue."

This narrative was inclosed in the following letter to Sir Walter Scott, without date or signature.

SIR,—The occurrence just related happened to me twenty-six years ago.[1]   Helen Walker lies buried in the churchyard of Irongray, about six miles from Dumfries. I once proposed that a small monument should have been erected to commemorate so remarkable a character, but I now prefer leaving it to you to perpetuate her memory in a more durable form."

How ably Sir Walter fulfilled the task thus placed in his hands will be understood and appreciated by all who have read his glowing narratives of the journey and sufferings of Jeanie Deans in her venturous trip to London.

Miss Goldie afterwards favoured Sir Walter with the following particulars concerning Helen Walker, which had been obtained by her mother :—

" Mrs. Goldie endeavoured to collect further particulars of Helen Walker, particularly concerning her journey to London, but found this nearly impossible, as the natural dignity of her character and a high sense of family respectability made her so indissolubly connect her sister's misfortune with her own exertions, that none of her neighbours durst ever question her upon the subject. One old woman, a distant relation of Helen's, who is still living, says she worked one harvest with her, but that she

---

[1] The introduction to the *Heart of Midlothian*, in which this letter appears, is dated 'Abbotsford, 1818.'

never ventured to ask her about her sister's trial, or her journey to London. 'Helen,' she added, 'was a lofty body, and used a high style o' language.' The same old woman says 'that every year Helen received a cheese from her sister, who lived at Whitehaven, and that she always sent a liberal portion of it to herself, or to her father's family. This fact, though trivial in itself, strongly marks the affection subsisting between the two sisters, and the complete conviction on the mind of the criminal that her sister had acted solely from high principle, not from any want of feeling, which another small but characteristic trait will further illustrate. A gentleman, a relation of Mrs. Goldie's, who happened to be travelling in the north of England, on coming to a small inn was shown into a parlour by the female servant, who, after cautiously shutting the door said, 'Sir, I'm Nelly Walker's sister.' Thus practically showing that she considered her sister as better known by her high conduct, than even herself by a different kind of celebrity.

"Mrs. Goldie was extremely anxious to have a tombstone, and an inscription upon it, erected in Irongray Churchyard; and if Sir Walter Scott will condescend to write the last, a little subscription could be easily raised in the immediate neighbourhood, and Mrs. Goldie's wish be thus fulfilled."

In answer to this modest request Sir Walter wrote:—

"It is scarcely necessary to add that the request of Miss Goldie will be most willingly complied with, and without the necessity of any tax upon the public. Nor is there much occasion to repeat how much the author conceives himself obliged to his unknown correspondent, who thus supplied him with a theme affording such a pleasant view of moral dignity of virtue, though unaided by birth, beauty, or talent. If the picture has suffered in the execution it is from the failure of the author's powers to present in detail the same simple and striking portrait exhibited to him."

A monument was accordingly afterwards erected, bearing the following inscription :—

This stone was erected
by the author of Waverley
To the memory of

HELEN WALKER,

Who died in the year of God, MDCCXCI.
This humble individual
practised in real life
the virtues
with which fiction has invested
the imaginary character of

JEANIE DEANS.

Refusing the slightest departure
from veracity,
even to save the life of her sister;
She nevertheless showed her
kindness and fortitude
in rescuing her
from the severity of the law,
at the expense of personal exertions
which the time rendered as dif.icult
as the motive was laudable.

Respect the grave of poverty,
when combined with the love of truth
and dear affection.

Jeanie Deans is recompensed by her biographer for the trials through which he leads her, with a full measure of earthly comfort, for few novelists dare venture to make virtue its own reward; yet the following reflection shows him to have felt how little the ordinary course of Providence is in accordance with man's natural wishes, and his expectations of a splendid temporal reward of goodness:— "That a character so distinguished for her undaunted love of virtue lived and died in poverty, if not want, serves only to show us how insignificant in the sight of Heaven are our principal objects of ambition upon earth."

GRACE DARLING.

GRACE HORSELEY DARLING was born at Longstone, one of
the Farne Islands, off the coast of Northumberland, on
the 15th of November, 1816, her father, William Darling,
being keeper of the lighthouse on the island. As a girl
she was quick and intelligent, and the education which
she received, chiefly from her father and mother, a superior
well-educated couple, combined with a natural love of
knowledge and a retentive memory, enabled her to spend
her youth on the lonely island in such a manner as to
make her life pleasant, and to be a source of real comfort
to her parents and the other members of the family. As
she grew up, and her brothers and sisters went out from
Longstone into the world, her father would scarcely allow
himself to be without her presence, and ultimately she was
the only one left to cheer the hearts of her father and
mother.

As Grace advanced she was known by friends who
visited the island, and by the neighbours on the mainland,
as a most amiable and intelligent young woman. William
Howitt, the well-known author, who paid a visit to the
lighthouse after our heroine had become famous, thus
described her:—"She had the sweetest smile I have ever
seen in a person of her station and appearance. You perceive that she is a thoroughly good creature, and that
under her modest exterior lies a spirit of the most exalted
devotion, so entire, that daring is not so much a quality
of her nature as that of the most perfect sympathy with

suffering or endangered humanity, swallowing up and annihilating everything like fear or self-consideration." Describing the rocky residence of the Darlings the same author says, " It was like the rest of these desolate isles, all of dark whinstone, cracked in every direction, and worn with the action of winds, waves, and tempests, since the world began.   On the greatest part of it there was not a blade of grass, nor a grain of earth, but bare and iron-like stone, crusted round the coast as far as high-water mark with limpet and still smaller shells.   We ascended wrinkled hills of black stone, and descended into worn and dismal dells of the same, into some of which, where the tide got entrance, it came pouring and roaring in raging whiteness, and churning the loose fragments of the whinstone into round pebbles, and piled them up into deep crevices with sea-weeds, like great round ropes and heaps of fucus.   Over our heads screamed hundreds of hovering birds, the gull mingling his laughter most wildly."

Such was the home of Grace Darling; shut out from the companionship of children of her own age, she grew up to womanhood a veritable child of the rock, for whom even the raging tempest had few terrors, save when the island shores and the near sea margin were strewn with wrecks, and death and devastation were all around.   The first sixteen years of her life passed unmarked beyond the ordinary course of events.   She now lingered on the verge of girlhood, and the simple and artless girl was fast emerging into a thoughtful and noble woman.

Owing to the dangerously exposed position of the Long-stone lighthouse the father of our heroine had very fre-quently, during the winter season especially, to render assistance to vessels in distress, either by piloting them safely through the numerous rocks and islands, or by receiving and succouring crews which were compelled to resort to his island for shelter. Of course, in all cases where possible, Grace took her share in aiding her father in his dangerous but noble duty, and so early became habituated to such scenes and circumstances; while in the management of a boat she is said to have displayed a dexterity and daring which few of the sterner sex could equal, and none surpass.

It is unnecessary here to recount the minor incidents in the career of Grace Darling, not that they are unworthy of record, but that the space at our command will not suffice for doing so, and also that the crowning effort of her life—the rescue of the passengers of the *Forfarshire* steamer—overshone them all, and it was by this act of unparalleled bravery alone that her name became the property of history, and her fame as the " Heroine of the Farne Isles" became a household word throughout the whole civilized world.

The following account of that disastrous shipwreck is substantially correct, and is compiled from narratives published immediately afterwards by the local and general newspapers when the incidents were fresh in the memory of every person :—

The *Forfarshire*, a steam-vessel of about three hundred tons burden, under the command of John Humble, sailed from Hull for Dundee on the evening of Wednesday, the 5th of September, 1838, with a valuable cargo of bale goods and sheet-iron; and having on board about twenty cabin and the same number of steerage passengers, Captain Humble and his wife, ten seamen, four firemen, two engineers, two coal-trimmers, and two stewards—in all, about sixty-three persons.

The vessel was only two years old, but her boilers were in a state of inefficiency. Previous to leaving Hull they had been examined, and a small leak closed up; but when off Flamborough Head the leakage reappeared and continued for about six hours, not, however, to what was considered a serious extent, as the pumps were able to keep the vessel dry. But after that time the leakage increased so greatly that two of the fires were extinguished. These, however, were relighted after the boilers had been partially repaired. The progress of the vessel was of course retarded, and three steam-vessels passed her before she had proceeded far. The unusual bustle on board the *Forfarshire* in consequence of the state of the boilers attracted the notice of several of the passengers; and Mrs. Dawson, a steerage passenger, who was one of the survivors, stated that even before the vessel left Hull, so strong was her impression, from indications on board, that all was not right, that if her husband had come down to the steamer in time she would have returned with him on shore.

In this disabled state the vessel proceeded on her voyage, and passed through the Fairway, between the Farne Island and the land, about six o'clock on Thursday evening. She entered Berwick Bay about night, the sea running high and the wind blowing strong from the north. From the motion of the vessel the leak increased to such a degree that the firemen could not keep the fires burning. Two men were then employed to pump water into the boilers, but it escaped through the leak as fast as they pumped it in. About ten o'clock she was off St. Abb's Head, the storm rapidly increasing. The engines soon became useless, and the engineers and fire-men were unable to work. There being great danger of drifting ashore, the sails were hoisted fore and aft, and the ship put about in order to keep her before the wind, and keep her off the land. No attempt was made to anchor. The vessel soon became unmanageable, and the tide setting in strongly to the south, she proceeded in that direction. It rained heavily during the whole time, and the fog was so dense that it became impossible to tell in what direction they were going. At length breakers were discovered close to leeward, and the Farne lights, which about the same period became visible, left no doubt as to the imminent peril of all on board. The captain vainly attempted to avert the catastrophe by running the vessel between the island and the mainland; she would not answer her helm, and was completely at the mercy of a furious sea. Between three and four o'clock she struck bow foremost on the rock, the ruggedness of which is such that, in periods when it is dry, it is scarcely possible for a person to stand erect upon it; and the edge which struck the *Forfarshire* descends sheer down a hundred fathoms deep or more.

> " Upheaved the ponderous ship, then downward flung;
> The shivering seamen to the bulwarks clung.
> Another plunge, she struck the solid rock—
> Her beams give way, her timbers feel the shock.
> Now all confusion, bustle, and dismay,
> All hands are urged on deck to find their way."

But, alas! many never reached the deck; of those who did, many were instantly swept into the fathomless deep.

At this juncture a portion of the crew, intent on self-preservation, lowered the larboard quarter boat and left the ship. In the investigations which afterwards took place the conduct of these men was severely commented upon.

The stroke of the vessel on the rock was regarded as the signal of death. The scene on board became of the most heartrending kind. The master lost all self-pos-

session; and his wife sought by the most heartrending
cries, that protection which, alas! he could not extend.
The cries of females on deck mingled with the roaring of
the ocean, and the screams of the wild fowl disturbed
from their resting-place; whilst the men, clinging to the
vessel, awaited in silence their inevitable fate.

Most of the cabin passengers were below, and many of
them asleep in their berths. As soon as the vessel struck
the steward gave the alarm, but one passenger only, a
Mr. Ritchie, got off. On being awoke he rose instantly
and rushed upon deck; from whence, observing the
sailors leaping into the boat, he, with an extraordinary
effort, by means of a rope swung himself into it, and thus
succeeded in preserving his life. The uncle and aunt of
Ritchie made a desperate effort to get into this boat just
as it was leaving the wreck, and in endeavouring to do so
they fell into the sea and perished before his eyes. He
had nothing on all the time he was in the boat but a
shirt and a pair of trousers, and his employment whilst
in it was baling out the water with a pair of shoes. The
escape of the boat was remarkable. There was only one
outlet by which it could avoid being dashed to pieces by
the breakers against the island, and that outlet was taken
without the parties being aware of it. The boat's crew
passed through the mighty current uninjured, and after
being exposed to the tempest all night were picked up
about eight o'clock on Saturday morning by a Montrose
sloop, and carried into Shields. There were nine persons
thus saved by this boat.

Returning to the vessel: very soon after the first
shock an immense wave struck her on the quarter, and
raising her off the rock allowed her immediately after
to fall violently down upon it, the sharp edge striking
her about midships; and scarcely three minutes after the

few survivors rushed upon deck a second shock separated
her into two parts—the stern, quarter-deck, and cabin
being instantly carried away, with all upon them, through
a tremendous current (dangerous even in temperate
weather) called the Piper Gat, which runs between the
islands with the rapidity of six miles an hour, and in
tempestuous weather becomes terrific. The fore part of
the vessel remained fast on the rock. The captain stuck
to the wreck till washed overboard with his wife, when
both perished.

The situation of the few passengers who remained on
the fore part of the vessel was now perilous in the extreme.
Placed on a small rock surrounded by the sea, which
threatened to engulf them, and their companions having
just before been swept away before them, they were
clinging to life whilst all hope of relief was sinking within
them, and crying for help whilst the tempestuous billows
drowned their feeble shrieks and defied their futile efforts
to escape.

The unhappy sufferers, nine in number (five of the
crew and four passengers), remained in their dreadful
situation till daybreak, exposed to the buffetings of the
waters, and fearful that every rising wave would sweep
the fragment of the wreck on which they stood into the
heaving deep.

At daybreak, however, their cries were heard. The
shouts of distress fell upon the ear of Grace Darling, who,
with her father, occupied the outer lighthouse. There, in
that solitary place, she listened, and scarcely knowing
whether the sounds proceeded from fancy or from a real
source, she awakened her father, and at daybreak on the
7th they descried the wreck. A mist hovered over the
island; and though the wind had somewhat abated, the
sea, which even in the calmest weather is never at rest

amongst the gorges of these iron rocks, still raged furiously.
Through the dim mist, with the aid of a telescope, the
figures of the sufferers were seen clinging to the wreck
at about half a mile distance.   But who would dare to
tempt the raging abyss that intervened, with the hope of
succouring them!   It is said Darling himself shrank from
the attempt—not so his gallant daughter! and at her
earnest solicitation the boat was launched, with the
assistance of her mother; and the noble Grace with
matchless intrepidity seized the oar and entered the boat.
This was enough; the father followed, and, with the
assistance of his daughter, conducted the frail skiff over
the boisterous billows.

At one time the boat was far aloof on a mountain of
waters, at another lost in a great watery vale.   How
bravely Grace struggled, how nobly she pulled at the car,
the foam splashing in her face, the boat heaving, tossing,
and reeling.   By a dangerous and desperate effort the
father was landed on the rock; and the frail coble, to
prevent its being dashed to pieces, was rapidly rowed
back into the awful abyss of waters, and kept afloat by
the skilfulness and dexterity of this noble-minded young
woman.

Had it not been ebb-tide the boat could not have passed
between the islands, and the Darlings were perfectly
aware that the tide would be flowing on their return,
when all the strength they could exert would be insuffi-
cient to bring their boat back to the lighthouse; and but
for getting the assistance of the sailors from the rock,
they themselves would have had to remain beside the
sufferers till the return of the tide.

The whole of the survivors, however, were taken from
the wreck and conveyed to the lighthouse, where for
three days and three nights the Darlings ministered to

their wants, the weather being of such a nature as to prevent their leaving the island.

This perilous achievement, unexampled in the feats of female heroism, was witnessed by the survivors in silent wonder, and one old sailor could not restrain the tears from flowing down his weather-beaten cheeks when he beheld the boat manned only by two persons, and one of these a young woman of slender appearance, buffeting the storm, and perilling her own life for their preservation.

The weather, we have said, being so boisterous, the mainland could not be reached till Sunday, and during the whole of that time the attentions of the young heroine were indefatigable. The entire number saved (out of a supposed total of 63), including those who escaped in the boat, was eighteen, of whom thirteen belonged to the vessel, and five were passengers.

The wreck of the steamer was observed from North Sunderland, when signals were hoisted and guns fired immediately; but men could not be found on account of the terrible storm to venture off in the life-boat. But after the lapse of some hours seven persons volunteered their services, and set out in a four-oared coble; one of these, by a remarkable coincidence, being Brooks Darling, brother to Grace. The boat shipped several seas during her perilous voyage, and on their way spoke the *Liverpool*, a steam-vessel of London, going north, and requested the captain to proceed to the wreck, offering at the same time to pilot the vessel to a few yards off the lee of the rock in seven fathoms water. The captain, however, refused, and the men in the coble, after much exertion, succeeded in reaching the wreck; but they found only dead bodies, and property of little value. The storm raged with unabated fury, and in attempting to return they were compelled to put in at the Longstone Light-

house, which they reached with difficulty, and were
obliged to remain for two days and two nights in a tem-
porary building, the waves occasionally bursting in and
driving them for shelter to the lighthouse tower, which
was occupied by the Darlings and the persons they had
saved from the wreck.

One of the most heartrending circumstances connected
with this melancholy event occurred during the night the
survivors were on the rock. The vessel became a total
wreck in less than a quarter of an hour after she struck;
and those who were fortunate enough to get on the rock
suffered severely from the cold, and from the heavy seas
which washed over them at intervals; and from continued
exertions they were soon reduced to a state of complete
exhaustion. The most agonizing spectacle was that of
Mrs. Dawson, with her two children, a boy and a girl,
eight and eleven years of age, firmly grasped in her hand;
there she held them in the agonies of despair, long after
the buffetings of the waves, which drove them to and fro,
had deprived them of existence. She was severely in-
jured, and remained at Bamborough for a time, unable to
proceed homewards. All hope of deliverance had fled,
and the unfortunate sufferers began to consider how to
relieve their sufferings if exposed through another night,
when the boat of the intrepid Darlings hove in sight.

The heroic courage and contempt of danger exhibited
by this simple island maiden and her aged father won the
admiration of every heart susceptible of noble and generous emotion.

No sooner had the newspapers heralded the bravery of
this wonderful girl than the whole nation stood amazed.
All eyes were turned to the lonely lighthouse, which became a centre of attraction to curious and sympathizing
thousands, amongst all grades and shades of society, includ-

ing many of the wealthy and the great, who bore testimony to their admiration of the young heroine by the substantial presents they made to her.   A public subscription was raised, by which she was presented with more than £700. The President of the Royal Humane Society sent her a very handsome silver teapot, and the Society itself presented her with a most flattering vote of thanks.   Her praise was sounded by all ranks throughout the country; and numbers of her portraits and pictures of the rescue were published and eagerly bought up.   To such a state of enthusiasm, indeed, was the nation wrought, that one of the London theatres offered her £800 for merely going for eight nights to sit in a boat upon the stage, while the performance progressed.   But she was not a woman to expose herself to the gaze of the curious for worldly gain, and she declined the offer, not without a feeling of indignation at its being made.

While congratulations and more substantial recognitions were being freely sent, Grace and her father were agreeably surprised to receive an intimation from the Duchess of Northumberland to the effect that she desired their presence at Alnwick Castle.   This caused quite a sensation in the lighthouse; and the prospect of such an interview almost overcame the modest Grace.   She had contended with the billows, but in her simplicity and inexperience of all but island life she naturally shrunk from such publicity.

At length, however, she was prevailed upon to obey the summons, and received a most hearty welcome.

.The duchess informed her that the fame of their late conduct had reached the circle of the Court, and such was the admiration excited in the breast of Her Majesty, Queen Victoria, that she had been graciously commissioned to convey to Grace Darling a token of approbation from the hands of royalty. The astonished maid could only, by repeated curtsies and grateful looks, express the feelings of thankfulness with which her heart overflowed.

The duchess then placed in the hands of Grace a packet containing the present of Her Majesty, to which was added a valuable gift from the duke and herself.

The public seldom allow great meritorious actions to go unrewarded. On this occasion an ardent desire had taken possession of the public mind to offer a substantial reward; and with this object subscriptions were immediately commenced throughout the kingdom. His Grace the Duke of Northumberland took a lively interest in the efforts, taking charge of the subscriptions, and giving Grace substantial advice in respect to them.

The Royal National Institution for the Preservation of Life from Shipwreck voted the silver medal of the institution to Mr. Darling and his daughter, and also subscribed the sum of £10 in aid of the Darling Fund.

The Directors of the Glasgow Humane Society sent to Grace their honorary silver medal, to mark the high sense entertained by them of her meritorious conduct. It bears the following inscription:—

"Presented by the Directors of the Glasgow Humane Society to Miss Grace Horseley Darling, in admiration of her dauntless and heroic conduct in saving (along with her father) the lives of nine persons from the wreck of the *Forfarshire* Steamer, 7th September, 1838."

Among the poetic effusions which celebrated the achievement and virtues of our heroine, none were more appreciated by Grace and her father than the following eulogistic stanzas which were written by Wordsworth:—

" Among the dwellers in the silent fields
    The natural heart is touched, and public way,

And crowded street, resound with ballad strains,
Inspired by one, whose very name bespeaks
Favour divine, exalting human love,
Whom, since her birth on bleak Northumbria's coast,
Known but to few, but prized as far as known,
A single act endears to high and low
Through the whole land—to manhood, moved in spite
Of the world's freezing cares—to generous youth—
To infancy, that lisps her praise—and age,
Whose eye reflects it, glistering through a tear
Of tremulous admiration. Such true fame
Awaits her now; but, verily, good deeds
Do not imperishable record find
Save in the rolls of heaven, where hers may live,
A theme for angels, when they celebrate
The high-soul'd virtues which forgetful earth
Has witnessed. Oh! that winds and waves could speak
Of things which their united power call'd forth
From the pure depths of her humanity!
A maiden gentle, yet, at duty's call,
Firm and unflinching as the lighthouse reared
On the island rock, her lonely dwelling-place,
Or like the invincible rock itself that braves,
Age after age, the hostile elements,
As when it guarded holy Cuthbert's cell.

All night the storm had raged, nor ceased, nor paused,
When, as day broke, the maid, through misty air,
Espies far off a wreck, amid the surf,
Beating on one of those disastrous isles.
Half of a vessel!—half—no more! The rest
Had vanished, swallowed up with all that there
Had for the common safety striven in vain,
Or thither thronged for refuge. With quick glance
Daughter and sire through optic glass discern,
Clinging about the remnant of this ship,
Creatures—how precious in the maiden's sight!
For whom, belike, the old man grieves still more
Than for their fellow sufferers engulphed
Where every parting agony is hushed,
And hope and fear mix not in further strife.

"But courage, father! let us out to sea—
A few may yet be saved." The daughter's words,
Her earnest tone and look, beaming with faith,
Dispel the father's doubts; nor do they lack
The noble-minded mother's helping hand
To launch the boat; and with her blessing cheer'd,
And inwardly sustained by silent prayer,
Together they put forth, father and child!
Each grasps an oar, and, struggling, on they go—
Rivals in effort; and, alike intent
Here to elude and there surmount, they watch
The billows lengthening, mutually cross'd
And shattered, and regathering their might,
As if the wrath and trouble of the sea
Were by the Almighty's sufferance prolong'd,
That woman's fortitude—so tried, so proved—
May brighten more and more!

                              True to that mark,
They stem the current of that perilous gorge,
Their arms still strengthening with the strengthening heart,
Though danger, as the wreck is neared, becomes
More imminent.   Not unseen do they approach;
And rapture, with varieties of fear
Incessantly conflicting, thrills the frame
Of those who, in that dauntless energy,
Foretaste deliverance; but the least perturb'd
Can scarcely trust his eyes, when he perceives
That of the pair—tossed on the waves to bring
Hope to the hopeless, to the dying, life—
One is a woman, a poor earthly sister;
Or, be the visitant other than she seems!
A guardian spirit sent from pitying heaven,
In woman's shape!   But why prolong the tale,
Casting weak words amid a host of thoughts
Arm'd to repel them?   Every hazard faced,
And difficulty mastered, with resolve
That no one breathing should be left to perish,
This last remainder of the crew are all
Placed in the little boat, then o'er the deep
Are safely borne, landed upon the beach.

And, in fulfilment of God's mercy, lodged
Within the sheltering lighthouse. Shout, ye waves!
Pipe a glad song of triumph, ye fierce winds!
Ye screaming sea-mews, in the concert join!
And would that some immortal voice,
Fitly attuned to all that gratitude
Breathes out from flock or couch through pallid lips
Of the survivors, to the clouds might bear—
(Blended with praise of that parental love,
Pious and pure, modest, and yet so brave,
Though young, so wise, though meek, so resolute)—
Might carry to the clouds and to the stars,
Yea, to celestial choirs, GRACE DARLING'S name!

But, alas! with all these honours and well-deserved rewards which followed the noble deed of Grace Darling,
she was destined to be not long for this world.   Her con-
stitution had never been a strong one, and during the
year 1841 she exhibited symptoms of declining health.
It soon became apparent that she was suffering from con-
sumption; and towards the end of that year, acting on
advice, she left Longstone to reside in Bamborough, where
she received, from the Duke and Duchess of Northumberland and other friends, every attention that wealth could
procure, and kindness suggest.   She was removed to
Alnwick at the request of the duke, in order that she
might have the best advice, but all was of no avail, and it
soon became evident that she was at the portals of death.
Her father being anxious that she should return to her
family, she was again removed to her sister's house at
Bamborough, where she arrived only ten days before her
death.

Before she died she expressed a strong desire to see as
many of her relatives as the nature of their employments
would permit to visit; and in the calmest manner gave to
each some token of remembrance, and assured them she was

only changing this life for one more desirable; that to
remain here was to be subject to trouble and sickness, but
to die was to be with Christ, her Saviour.   On the 20th
of October, 1842, with the most complete resignation, she
yielded her spirit up to God without a murmur.   At her
death she had barely attained the age of twenty-five years.
Her remains were interred in Bamborough churchyard,
where a tombstone marks their resting-place.

"Blessed are the dead who die in the Lord."   In truth
it may be said of Grace Darling, "Though dead she yet
speaketh."   "Her heroism speaks, her generosity and
kindly nature speak, her religion speaks, her general
character speaks, and her manner of dying speaks; and,
using the old simile, just as the stone thrown into the
pond causes the ripples to move over the whole face of
the water to the shore, so the lessons from her life, simple,
yet glorious, shall never die."

IDA LEWIS,

THE LIGHTHOUSE KEEPER OF RHODE ISLAND.

THE example of Grace Darling has borne good fruit. The very year of her death a child was born in America, who was destined to distinguish herself in a similar manner. The story of her life, so far as yet experienced—for we understand that the heroine of Newport is still alive—is briefly as follows.

In 1842, when the buds were opening to the showers of spring, Ida Lewis was born. Her father, Hosea Lewis, formerly a revenue pilot, was appointed, in 1853, Keeper of the Lime Rock Lighthouse. The rock commands the widest view of the harbour of Newport, and upon it the keeper lived alone for three years and a half, when a stroke of paralysis disabled him from all work. From that time his eldest daughter Ida became the mainstay of the family. She nursed her father, lightened her mother's toil, watched over her younger sister Harriet, rowed her brothers Rudolf and Hosea to school, eked out her father's slender wage with her needle; and went to the rescue of imperilled persons, risking her own life in the hazardous venture.

In September, 1859, when only seventeen years of age, Ida gave the first proof of her daring courage. Four gay young fellows, all about eighteen or twenty years of age, one from Philadelphia and the others from Newport, and all sons of wealthy gentlemen, went out for an evening sail. One of the number, in thoughtless braggadocio

climbed up the mast and upset the boat half a mile from
the nearest shore.   None of them could swim that distance
—night was rapidly overcovering the sky—the capsized
boat was too light to support them all, and they were
ruefully awaiting the consequences of their mad frolic
when the keeper's daughter, spying their danger through
the dusk, put out in her skiff, single-handed, and rescued
them all from their impending fate.

During an intervening period of ten years Ida Lewis
has saved five other lives.   One cold and wintry February
day three intoxicated sailors stole a boat and set out
across the harbour for Fort Adams.   By some drunken
recklessness they stove a hole in the bottom of the boat,
and it began to fill rapidly.   Two of the men succeeded
in swimming ashore, but the third clung to the submerged
boat and tried to paddle with his feet across the harbour.
When discovered and picked up by Ida he was insensible
with cold, and it was with great difficulty that she released
the deathlike clutch with which he held on to the bottom
of the upturned boat.

In 1867 a valuable sheep escaped from those who had
charge of it, leaped off one of the Newport wharves, and
started to swim round the harbour.   Three men who
went in pursuit along the shore, finding a skiff, put off in
it to endeavour to recover the animal.   But a fierce gale,
blowing from the north-west, was too much for them;
the boat began to swamp rapidly; they could not regain
the shore, and were staring death in the face, when Ida
rowed to their relief, carried them and their skiff to land,
and then went out and succeeded in recovering the sheep.

One of the latest of Ida's feats of intrepidity was accomplished on a stormy afternoon of March, a few years
ago.   The rain fell in blinding torrents, and the gale
drove the waves across Newport harbour with a fury that

taxed the full strength and skill of the most experienced boatmen. In the midst of this storm a reckless boy, who had somehow or other obtained possession of one of the most unsafe sailing-boats in the harbour of Newport, afterwards known as the "Soldier-Drowner," succeeded in persuading two soldiers to allow him to carry them from the city to Fort Adams, where they were stationed. Anxious to escape the dreary three-mile journey by land, and believing in the boy's capability to manage the boat, the soldiers accepted his offer, and had made half the trip in safety when a sudden squall struck the sail. The startled boy jammed the helm in the wrong direction, and in an instant the boat was capsized and tossing on the big and broken waves. For a long half-hour the soldiers and the boy clung to the keel, and wrestled against the blinding rain and the wild waves with the agonized strength of despair; but finally the boy's strength was exhausted, and with a wailing cry he sank and was seen no more. Fast paralysing with cold and bereft of hope, the two soldiers saw no choice left but to clasp each other in a last embrace and sink to a mutual grave, when suddenly from the Lime Rock, half a mile away, a little boat shot out, driven by rapid strokes towards the drowning men. Ida and her young brother plied the oars. Hope rose in the breasts of the soldiers, but sank back again on seeing in the boat only a slender youth and still more slender young woman. The boy was almost reaching over the side to grasp the nearest soldier when Ida called out, "Stop, Hosey! we shall be upset that way."

She turned the boat with a well-timed stroke, and one man was drawn safely in over the stem; another backward pull, another lift, and the next minute the frail craft with its freight of rescued life was cleaving its way back to the rock again.

The personal appearance of Ida Lewis is thus described in an influential newspaper printed in New York in 1876 :—

"This Newport heroine scarcely attains the average height of women, is remarkably slender, and would be thought much nearer twenty than twenty-seven. No one can talk to her without believing her to be as unselfish as she is fearless, and the fame her heroism has created does not in the least excite a feeling of vanity in her."

THE END.

BLACKIE & SON'S

BOOKS FOR YOUNG PEOPLE.

New Series for Season 1884.

BY G. A. HENTY.

WITH CLIVE IN INDIA:
OR THE BEGINNINGS OF AN EMPIRE.

BY SHEER PLUCK:
A TALE OF THE ASHANTI WAR.

BY G. MANVILLE FENN.

THE GOLDEN MAGNET:
A TALE OF THE LAND OF THE INCAS.

BY ASCOTT R. HOPE.

THE WIGWAM AND THE WAR-PATH:
STORIES OF THE RED INDIANS.

BY JOHN C. HUTCHESON.

PICKED UP AT SEA:
OR THE GOLD MINERS OF MINTURNE CREEK.

By ALICE BANKS.

CHEEP AND CHATTER:
OR LESSONS FROM FIELD AND TREE.

By LEWIS HOUGH.

DR. JOLLIFFE'S BOYS:
A TALE OF WESTON SCHOOL.

By HENRY FRITH.

JACK O' LANTHORN:
A TALE OF ADVENTURE.

By KATE WOOD.

A WAIF OF THE SEA:
OR THE LOST FOUND.

By ROSA MULHOLLAND.

HETTY GRAY:
OR NOBODY'S BAIRN.

By GEORGE SAND.
TRANSLATED FROM THE FRENCH BY MRS. CORKRAN.

THE WINGS OF COURAGE: AND THE CLOUD-SPINNER.

By ANNIE E. ARMSTRONG.

MADGE'S MISTAKE:
A RECOLLECTION OF GIRLHOOD.

Twenty-third Thousand, medium 8vo, cloth elegant, 7s. 6d.

THE UNIVERSE:

OR THE INFINITELY GREAT AND THE INFINITELY LITTLE. A Sketch of Contrasts in Creation, and Marvels revealed and explained by Natural Science. By F. A. POUCHET, M.D. Illustrated by 273 Engravings on wood, of which 56 are full-page size. 7th Edition, medium 8vo, cloth elegant, gilt edges, 7s. 6d.; also full morocco, blind tooled.

The object of this Work is to inspire and extend a taste for natural science. It is not a learned treatise, but a simple study. The title adopted indicates that the author has gathered from creation at large, often contrasting the smallest of its productions with the mightiest.

Neptune's Cup.

"We can honestly commend this work, which is admirably, as it is copiously, illustrated."—*Times.*

"As interesting as the most exciting romance, and a great deal more likely to be remembered to good purpose."—*Standard.*

"Scarcely any book in French or in English is so likely to stimulate in the young an interest in the physical phenomena."—*Fortnightly Review.*

"The volume, and it is a splendid one, will serve as a good pioneer to more exact studies."—*Saturday Review.*

WITH CLIVE IN INDIA:

Or the Beginnings of an Empire. By G. A. Henty, author of "Facing Death," "Under Drake's Flag," "The Young Buglers," &c. With 12 full-page Illustrations printed in black and tint. In crown 8vo, cloth elegant, bevelled boards, olivine edges, 6s.

The period between the landing of Clive as a young writer in India and the close of his career was critical and eventful in the extreme. At its commencement the English were traders existing on sufferance of the native princes. At its close they were masters of Bengal and of the greater part of Southern India. The Author has given a full and accurate account of the historical events of that stirring time, and battles and sieges follow each other in rapid succession, while he combines with his narrative a tale of daring and adventure, which gives a lifelike interest to the volume.

THE GOLDEN MAGNET:

A Tale of the Land of the Incas. By Geo. Manville Fenn, author of "In the King's Name," "Nat the Naturalist," "Off to the Wilds," &c. With 12 full-page pictures printed in black and tint. In crown 8vo, cloth elegant, bevelled boards, olivine edges, 6s.

This is a story of adventure such as will be sure to be attractive to most lads of quick imagination, and like most of Mr. Fenn's stories it contains genuine descriptive passages and accurate touches of natural history, which not only increase its interest but enhance its value. The tale is of a romantic lad who leaves home where his father conducts a failing business to seek his fortune in South America, first by finding his uncle, who is owner of a coffee plantation on the banks of the Orinoco; and secondly by endeavouring to discover some of that treasure which legends declare was ages ago hidden by the Peruvian rulers and the priests of that mysterious country, to preserve it from the Spanish invaders. The hero of the story is accompanied by a faithful companion, who, in the capacity both of comrade and henchman, does true service and shows the dogged courage of the English lad during the strange adventures which befall them. The plot of the story is simple, but the movement is rapid and full of strange excitement. There are few lads who will not follow it with keen enjoyment from beginning to end.

·UNDER DRAKE'S FLAG.

A Tale of the Spanish Main. By G. A. HENTY, author of "The Young Buglers," "The Cornet of Horse," "In Times of Peril," &c. Illustrated by 12 full-page Pictures printed in black and tint. Crown 8vo, cloth elegant, bevelled boards, price 6s.

"Under Drake's Flag," is a story of the days when England and Spain struggled for the supremacy of the sea, and England carried off the palm. The heroes of the story sail as lads with Drake in the expedition in which the Pacific Ocean was first seen by an Englishman from a tree-top on the Isthmus of Panama, and in his great voyage of circumnavigation. The historical portion of the story is absolutely to be relied upon, but this, although very useful to lads, will perhaps be less attractive than the great variety of exciting adventure through which the young adventurers pass in the course of their voyages.

"A stirring book of Drake's time, and just such a book as the youth of this maritime country are likely to prize highly."—*Daily Telegraph.*

IN THE KING'S NAME:

Or the Cruise of the *Kestrel*. By G. MANVILLE FENN, author of "Off to the Wilds," "Middy and Ensign," &c. Illustrated by 12 full-page Pictures printed in black and tint. Crown 8vo, cloth extra, bevelled boards, price 6s.

"In the King's Name" is a spirited story of the Jacobite times, concerning the adventures of Hilary Leigh, a young naval officer in the preventive service off the coast of Sussex, on board the *Kestrel*. Leigh is taken prisoner by the adherents of the Pretender, amongst whom is an early friend and patron who desires to spare the lad's life, but will not release him. The narrative is full of exciting and often humorous incident.

"Mr. Manville Fenn has already won a foremost place among writers of stories for boys. 'In the King's Name' is, we are inclined to think, the best of all his productions in this field. It has the great quality of always 'moving on'—adventure following adventure in constant succession."—*Daily News.*

"Told with the freshness and nerve which characterize all Mr. Fenn's writings and put him in the front rank of writers for boys."—*Standard.*

BY SHEER PLUCK:

A Tale of the Ashanti War. By G. A. HENTY, author of "Facing
Death," "Under Drake's Flag," "The March to Coomassie,"
&c. With 8 full-page Illustrations printed in black and tint.
In crown 8vo, cloth elegant, 5s.

The Ashanti Campaign seems but an event of yesterday, but it happened
when the generation now rising up were too young to have made themselves acquainted with its incidents. The author has woven, in a tale of
thrilling interest, all the details of the campaign, of which he was himself
a witness. His hero, after many exciting adventures in the interior, finds
himself at Coomassie just before the outbreak of the war, is detained a
prisoner by the king, is sent down with the army which invaded the British
Protectorate, escapes, and accompanies the English expedition on their
march to Coomassie.

THE WIGWAM AND THE WAR-PATH:

Stories of the Red Indians. By ASCOTT R. HOPE, author of
"Stories of Old Renown," "Buttons," &c. With 8 full-page
Pictures by GORDON BROWNE, printed in black and tint. In
crown 8vo, cloth elegant, 5s.

The interest taken by boys in stories of the North American Indians is
probably as keen as ever. At all events the works of Fenimore Cooper and
other writers about the red men and the wild hunters of the forests and
prairies are still among the most popular of boys' books. "The Wigwam
and the War-path" consists of stories of Red Indians which are none the
less romantic for being true. They are taken from the actual records of
those who have been made prisoners by the red men or have lived among
them, joining in their expeditions and taking part in their semi-savage but
often picturesque and adventurous life. The stories are conscientiously
told, and may be regarded as truthful pictures of scenes, events, and
occurrences which are full of interest not only for youthful readers, but in
a great measure for those of older growth.

STORIES OF OLD RENOWN.

Tales of Knights and Heroes. By Ascott R. Hope, Author of
"Spindle Stories," "The Old Tales of Chivalry," "Stories of
Long Ago," &c. &c. With nearly 100 Illustrations, of which
8 are full-page size, from Drawings by Gordon Browne.
Crown 8vo, cloth elegant, design on side, bevelled boards,
olivine edges, 5*s.*

A Series of the best of the Stories of Noble Knighthood and Old Romance, told in refined and simple language, and adapted to young readers. A book possessing remarkable attractions, especially for boys who love to hear of great deeds and enterprises of high renown.

"Ascott R. Hope here breaks new ground, and he deserves as much credit for his choice of subject as for his mode of treatment."—*Academy.*

"Ogier the Dane, Robert of Sicily, and other old-world heroes find their deeds embedded in beautiful type, and garnished with animated sketches by Gordon Browne. It is a charming gift-book."—*Land and Water.*

"Mr. Hope's style is quite in accord with his theme, and the simplicity with which he recounts these 'Stories of Old Renown' is by no means the least part of their attractiveness. Mr. Gordon Browne has furnished some excellent drawings to illustrate the text, in many of which we recognize the touch of his late father, Mr. Hablot K. Browne, and these drawings recall the time when 'Phiz' was at his freshest and his best."—*Pictorial World.*

FACING DEATH:

Or the Hero of the Vaughan Pit. A Tale of the Coal Mines. By G. A. HENTY, author of "In Times of Peril," &c. With 8 full-page Illustrations printed in black and tint. Crown 8vo, cloth elegant, price 5*s*.

"Facing Death" is a story with a purpose. It is intended to show that a lad who makes up his mind firmly and resolutely that he will rise in life, and who is prepared to face toil and ridicule and hardship to carry out his determination, is sure to succeed. The hero of the story, though only a colliery lad, is a character that boys will delight in. He is a typical British boy, dogged, earnest, generous, and though "shamefaced" to a degree, is ready to face death in the discharge of duty. His is a character for imitation by boys in every station, who will assuredly be intensely interested in the narrative.

"The tale is well written and well illustrated, and there is much reality in the characters."—*Athenæum.*

"If any father, godfather, clergyman, or schoolmaster is on the lookout for a good book to give as a present this season to a boy who is worth his salt, this is the book we would recommend."—*Standard.*

NAT THE NATURALIST:

Or a Boy's Adventures in the Eastern Seas. By GEO. MANVILLE FENN, author of "Off to the Wilds," &c. &c. Illustrated by 8 full-page Pictures executed in black and tint. Crown 8vo, cloth elegant, price 5*s*.

This is a pleasant story of a lad who, though he is brought up in a strictly quiet fashion by an aunt, has a great desire to go abroad to seek specimens in natural history, and has that desire gratified by an uncle who comes home from distant lands, whence he brings a beautiful collection. The boy Nat and his uncle Dick go on a voyage to the remoter islands of the Eastern seas, and their adventures there are told in a truthful and vastly interesting fashion, which will at once attract and maintain the earnest attention of young readers. The descriptions of Mr. Ebony, their black comrade, and of the scenes of savage life, are full of genuine humour.

"We can conceive of no more attractive present for a young naturalist."—*Land and Water.*

"A really delightful story of the adventures of a naturalist and his nephew in the Spice Islands."—*Truth.*

"The pictures, as we have remarked before of Messrs. Blackie's books, are far above the average, both in drawing and in reproduction."—*Academy.*

CHEEP AND CHATTER:

Or, Lessons from Field and Tree. By Alice Banks. With 50 Character Illustrations by Gordon Browne, of which four are full-page size. Small 4to, cloth, handsome design on cover, 3s. 6d.

About a dozen highly dramatic sketches or little stories, the actors in which are not men and women but birds, beasts, and insects. They are instructive, suited to the capacities of young people, and very amusing. The curious and laughable thing is the clever way in which mice, sparrows, and butterflies are made to act and talk just as one should imagine mice, sparrows, or butterflies would act and talk, and yet so wonderfully like men and women, or boys and girls, at the same time. We take an absorbing interest in the adventures of "Peepy" and "Cheepy," and "Birdie" and "Pecky," in the opinions they express and the characters they develop, just as if they were papas and mamas, and boys and girls; and whether we are in Fairy-land, or Mouse-land, or Bird-land, or in real Boy-and-girl-land, we cease to be sure, or, for the matter of that, to care. The character drawings, with which the book is profusely illustrated, are delightfully funny.

PICKED UP AT SEA:

Or the Gold Miners of Minturne Creek, and other Stories. By
JOHN C. HUTCHESON, author of "Caught in a Trap," "The
Penang Pirate," &c. With 6 full-page Pictures in Colour.
In crown 8vo, cloth extra, 3s. 6d.

"Picked up at Sea," is the story of a young English lad, rescued in mid
Atlantic from a watery grave, and taken out west by a party of gold diggers
to the wild regions of the Black Hills in Dakota. Here, after warring
with the elements during months of unceasing toil in their search for the
riches of the earth, and having the result of their indefatigable labour well
nigh torn from their grasp when on the verge of victory by a desperate
onslaught of Sioux braves under "Spotted Tail," success at last rewards
the efforts of the adventurous band and their protégé. The tale abounds
in exciting scenes and stirring incidents—about mining mishaps, shooting
exploits, and fights with the hostile Indians,—all tending to show that
pluck and perseverance when allied to a good cause invariably win in the
long run all the world over. The remainder of the book consists of spicy
yarns of life afloat and ashore by an "old salt," detailing adventures
amongst pirates and brigands, cut-throats and mutineers, in which heroism
comes out in relief as opposed to cowardice and cravenly fear; while the
dangers of the deep and the perils of those who "go down to the sea in
ships" are not forgotten.

DR. JOLLIFFE'S BOYS:

A Tale of Weston School. By LEWIS HOUGH, author of "Phil
Crawford," &c. With 6 full-page Pictures in black and tint.
In crown 8vo, cloth extra, 3s. 6d.

A story of school life which will be read with genuine interest, especially
as it exposes some of the dangers which even in these days of high instruc-
tion may beset lads who are ill instructed at home or have been thrown
among vicious or unscrupulous companions. The descriptions of some of
the characters of the boys at Dr. Jolliffe's are vivid and truthful,—that of
the worst boy being not too revolting, although it is necessarily painful as
conveying a very distinct impression which should be useful in warning
lads against giving way to overweening personal conceit and envy of the
achievements of others. Perhaps the best touch in the book is the subtle
description of the manner in which the best boy may exhibit weakness of
purpose and some meannesses under the influence of flattery and of tempo-
rary luxury. The narrative throughout is bright, easy, and lighted by
touches of humour, and the plot is so well sustained that the reader goes
on to the end without abatement of the keen interest which is provoked in
the very first chapter.

GARNERED SHEAVES.

A Tale for Boys. By Mrs. EMMA RAYMOND PITMAN, author of "Mission Life in Greece and Palestine," &c. With 4 full-page Illustrations printed in black and tint. Crown 8vo, cloth extra, price 3s. 6d.

This Tale gives in narrative form the history and adventures of a class of Sunday-school boys. Each boy's career is full of interest. In some chapters we are taken to America, during the civil war, and mingle in scenes relating to the battle-field; while, in other chapters, we listen to the quiet teachings of one of God's faithful servants, who strove to "garner sheaves for Christ." The wide difference between the honourable upright youth, and one who is clever and cunning, but dishonest, is here depicted by incidents from the life; and it is proved that "godliness hath promise of the life that now is," as well as of that which is to come. From this tale Sunday-school teachers may learn that their "labour shall not be in vain in the Lord."

" 'Garnered Sheaves' is a charming story of the after life and labours of two Sunday-school scholars whose careers were diverse in their character and influence." —*Christian Union.*

"The incidents are well depicted, and the characters are true to life. . . . We shall be glad of more such sheaves as these."—*Freeman.*

" It should be read by every youth who is leaving school and home for business."— *Literary World.*

MY GOVERNESS' LIFE:

Or Earning my Living. By Mrs. EMMA RAYMOND PITMAN, author of "Mission Life in Greece and Palestine," "Heroines of the Mission Field," "Vestina's Martyrdom," "Profit and Loss," &c. &c. With 4 full-page Illustrations. Cloth neat, 3s. 6d.

This Story, told in the first person, is largely concerned with a young woman cast upon the world by her father's death, and compelled to earn her living by the exercise of whatever talent she possesses. Some of the minor characters in the narrative are skilfully depicted, notably the old Cornish couple who figure in the little Methodist chapel; and the young man of science, who is shown to have missed his way in substituting science for faith in a personal God, but by painful chastening is recovered and led to the cross of Christ as a humble believer. Finally, he marries the heroine of the story, and turns out a good and useful man. The aged clergyman is a fine specimen of culture and Christian charity. The scenes of boarding-school life here depicted are full of vivacity and reality.

LIFE'S DAILY MINISTRY.

A Story of Everyday Service for Others. By Mrs. EMMA RAY-
MOND PITMAN, author of "Mission Life in Greece and Palestine," "Heroines of the Mission Field," "Vestina's Martyrdom," "Profit and Loss," &c. &c. With 4 full-page Illustrations
printed in black and tint. Crown 8vo, cloth neat, 3s. 6d.

A Story of self-sacrifice in various forms, and of some touching experiences of life. Some of the characters are very attractive, others very
repulsive; but all tend to show that true honour and happiness are to be
found in serving others, according to our capacity, and so imitating Him
"who went about doing good." Some experiences of a sincere and gifted,
but doubting youth, helpless through spinal disease and destined to early
death, and his attainment of faith, light, and peace, are peculiarly affecting. His brother, the medical student, is eventually brought back to faith
in his mother's God, after wandering very far in sin and folly. Olive
Forrester, the chief heroine of the story, presents an example of saintly
self-denial for the sake of her dead sister's children.

FLORENCE GODFREY'S FAITH.

A Story of Australian Life. By Mrs. EMMA RAYMOND PITMAN,
author of "Heroines of the Mission Field," &c. With 4 full-
page Illustrations printed in black and tint. Crown 8vo, cloth
extra, price 3s. 6d.

This Tale traces the career and adventures of a family who were forced
to leave Manchester during the time of the cotton famine, and seek a home
in Australian wilds. Florence, the central character of the story, is a very
lovely one; and in spite of girlish timidity, girlish fear, and natural shrinking, succeeds in raising a Christian church in the wilderness. The story
teaches the lesson of perseverance in well-doing, and shows how faithful
effort is rewarded.

"This is a clever, and what is better still, a good book, written with a freshness
and power which win the reader's sympathies, and carry the story along unflaggingly
to the close."—*Christian Globe.*

"A story which will be eagerly read by boys, and which can hardly fail to promote
the growth of a manly type of Christian character."—*Literary World.*

"This is a very interesting book, and a suitable present for young men or women.
The influence of the tale is pure and bracing."—*Freeman.*

"Mrs. Pitman's works are all to be prized for their ennobling character—pure,
elevating, interesting, and intellectual."—*Christian Union.*

BROTHER AND SISTER:

Or the Trials of the Moore Family. By ELIZABETH J. LYSAGHT,
author of "Nearer and Dearer," &c. With 6 full-page Illustrations in black and tint. Crown 8vo, cloth gilt, price 3s. 6d.

An interesting story for young people, showing by the narrative of the
vicissitudes and struggles of a family which has "come down in the world,"
and of the brave endeavours of its two younger members, how the pressure
of adversity is mitigated by domestic affection, mutual confidence, and
hopeful honest effort.

"A pretty story, and well told. The plot is cleverly constructed, and the moral
is excellent."—*Athenæum*.

"A charming story, admirably adapted for young people, which relates the brave
endeavours of the two youngest members of a family which has become reduced in
circumstances to mitigate the pressure of adversity."—*Society*.

DORA:

Or a Girl without a Home. By Mrs. R. H. READ, author of
"The Lawyer's Daughter," &c. &c. With 6 full-page Illustrations. Crown 8vo, cloth elegant, 3s. 6d.

The story of a friendless orphan girl, who is placed as pupil-teacher at
the school in which she was educated, but is suddenly removed by hard
and selfish relatives, who employ her as a menial as well as a governess.
Through a series of exciting adventures she makes discoveries respecting a
large property which is restored to its rightful owners, and at the same
time she secures her escape from her persecutors. The character of Dora
is a very sweet one, and the interest of the story is so sustained that it can
scarcely fail to please the reader.

UNRAVELLED SKEINS:

Or Tales for the Twilight. By GREGSON GOW. Illustrated by
four facsimile Designs in black and tint. Crown 8vo, cloth
elegant, price 3s. 6d.

"For a volume of neat stories carefully told commend us to this "—*Scotsman*.

MYTHS AND LEGENDS
OF ANCIENT GREECE AND ROME.

A Hand-book of Greek and Roman Mythology, by E. M. BERENS.
Illustrated from Antique Sculptures in a highly interesting
and instructive manner. Cloth elegant, price 3s. 6d.

"Written in a spirit of reverent sympathy and of well-sustained interest, while its
absolute purity should secure it a place in every family."—*Schoolmaster*.

JACK O' LANTHORN.

A Tale of Adventure. By HENRY FRITH, author of "Through
Flood, through Fire," "On the Wings of the Wind," &c.
With 4 full-page Illustrations, printed in black and tint. In
crown 8vo, cloth elegant, 2*s.* 6*d.*

This is a story which will be chiefly attractive to boys, and most boys
will read it with genuine interest, for it is told in a straightforward fashion
by the hero himself, a lad whose father was a Bristol tradesman in the
days when George the Third was king, and when "Jack the Painter" was
trying to set fire to the shipping in Government dockyards. The boy, who
tells his own history, gets into certain scrapes, and at the sea-coast makes
the acquaintance of Jack o' Lanthorn, a sailor and the keeper of a light-
ship. The lad and a companion accidentally drifting out to sea in an open
boat, discover in a singular manner the approach of the Spanish fleet, and
Jack o' Lanthorn accompanies the hero of the tale to report what they
have seen. Seized by a press-gang they are taken off to sea, and eventually take part in the defence of Gibraltar, and have some strange adventures
of their own. The author of the book has not only kept closely to the
history of the time, but has preserved the speech and manner of the
narrator. The episodes are striking, the plot full of peculiar interest, and
there have been few books published recently which so well represent the
spirit of those entertaining stories of the sea which made the reputation
of Marryat and of the author of "Tom Cringle's Log."

A WAIF OF THE SEA:

Or, the Lost Found. By KATE WOOD, author of "Lory Bell," &c.
With 4 full-page Illustrations. In small 8vo, cloth extra, 2*s.* 6*d.*

"A Waif of the Sea" is the kind of story which is likely to enlist the
sympathies of a large number of readers, for it deals very pathetically with
the sorrows and trials of children, and of mothers who are separated from
their children. With a gentle and affecting strain of religious feeling
which is neither too prominent nor too precise, the narrative is full of
human interest, and the lives and struggles of the people of a poor London
neighbourhood are well portrayed without unnecessary coarseness on the
one hand or a too romantic colouring on the other. The child-character
of "Little Birdie" and her short but affecting story will attract and
delight many readers, while the grown-up personages in the book are very
accurately and pleasingly drawn. One of the charms of the story is its
easy transition from town to country, and the freshness imparted to the
descriptive touches both of "Golden Square" and of the "Old Manor
House."

HETTY GRAY;

Or Nobody's Bairn. By ROSA MULHOLLAND, author of "Four Little Mischiefs," &c. With 4 full-page Illustrations. In small 8vo, cloth extra, 2s. 6d.

"Hetty Gray" is the story of a girl who, having been found as an infant by a villager, is brought up by his wife, and is a kind of general pet, till an accident causes a rich widow to adopt her, and spoil her by bringing her up in alternate indulgence and neglect. On the death of her adoptive mother Hetty, who is left unprovided for, is taken by the widow's relatives to be educated in the family as a dependant, but with a view to her gaining her livelihood as a governess, an event which is prevented by a rather remarkable discovery. The tale is carried on throughout with the simplicity but genuine effect which distinguishes Miss Mulholland's writing, and the interest felt by the reader in the struggles and trials of the foundling, and the gradual development of her character under circumstances often pathetic but frequently humorous, is maintained to the last.

THE BALL OF FORTUNE;

Or Ned Somerset's Inheritance. By CHARLES PEARCE, author of "Frank the Fisher-boy," &c. With 4 full-page Illustrations printed in black and tint. Crown 8vo, cloth extra, 2s. 6d.

A story of plot and character dealing with some out of the many scenes of London life, and founded on the strange bequest left by a sea captain, and the endeavours of some unscrupulous persons to obtain possession of it before the discovery of the true heir in the person of a neglected street Arab. The story is lively and attractive, and the incidents move so quickly that the attention of the reader is sustained throughout.

"It is a bright genial story, which boys will thoroughly enjoy. . . . The moral lies in the story itself, and is not administered in a succession of pious pills with sweet draughts of racy fiction between to take the taste away. We have seen few better stories for boys this season."—*Birmingham Daily Post.*

THE FAMILY FAILING.

By DARLEY DALE, author of "Little Bricks," "The Black Donkey," "A Tearful Victory," &c. &c. With 4 full-page Illustrations. Cloth elegant, 2s. 6d.

This is a lively and amusing account of a family, the members of which while they lived in affluence were remarkable for their discontent, but who, after the loss of fortune has compelled them to seek a more humble home in Jersey, become less selfish, and develop very excellent traits of character under the pressure of comparative adversity. Their escapades and narrow escapes from serious dangers form an exciting part of the narrative, which contains many pleasant episodes of life in the Channel Islands.

EPISODES OF THE SEA IN FORMER DAYS:

Records of Suffering and Saving. A Book for Boys. With engraved Title and Frontispiece. Cloth elegant, 2s. 6d.

Stories of shipwreck, famine, mutiny, and the other misfortunes which befall the mariner, will always be appreciated by those who love to read of deeds of daring, and to ponder on the lessons which may be drawn from them. This volume comprises narratives of occurrences which have become historical, such as the ever-memorable mutiny of the *Bounty*, and many others of equal interest.

EPISODES OF CAPTIVITY AND EXILE

In various Parts of Europe. A Book for Boys. With engraved Title and Frontispiece. Cloth elegant, 2s. 6d.

Captivity and Escape is at all times an attractive subject for youthful minds, presenting as it does to them scenes of adventurous daring, hardship, and suffering, calculated to excite their natural ardour and draw forth their ready sympathies. The tales embodied in this volume will be found to comprise those of the most fascinating description.

EPISODES OF HISTORY:

Stirring Incidents in the Lives of Men and Nations. A Book for Youth. With engraved Title and Frontispiece. Cloth elegant, 2s. 6d.

In the compilation of this volume the object has been to give a series of sketches stretching over a long term of time, rather than a finished picture of any definite period. These have been collected during an extensive course of reading, and the only attempt made at classification has been to place the articles in chronological order.

EPISODES OF DISCOVERY IN ALL AGES.

A Book for Youth. With engraved Title and Frontispiece. Cloth extra, 2s. 6d.

In this work will be found accounts of a few of the most famous discoverers and explorers of former days. The materials from which this volume has been compiled were gathered from scarce records and other trustworthy sources; and the whole forms a series of incidents of unexampled interest in the world's history.

EPISODES OF FOREIGN LIFE AND MANNERS,

And Pictures of Foreign Lands. A Book for Youth. With engraved Title and Frontispiece. Cloth elegant, 2s. 6d.

The object in this work is to whet the appetite rather than to satiate the mind of the readers—to create within them a desire to know more of the strange countries and peoples here mentioned.

EPISODES OF PERSONAL ADVENTURE

In Field, Flood, and Forest. A Book for Boys. With engraved Title and Frontispiece. Cloth elegant, 2s. 6d.

The incidents are wholly founded on the real experiences of those who figure in them. They have been carefully selected from numerous sources.

THE NEWSPAPER READER.

Selections from leading Journals of the Nineteenth Century on Events of the Day. By H. F. BUSSEY and T. W. REID. With engraved Frontispiece. F'cap 8vo, cloth extra, 2s. 6d.

"The idea of the book is admirable, and its execution is excellent. It is extremely interesting. It may be read not merely by young people, but by old ones, and they will find profit to themselves in its perusal. The work is well done."—*Scotsman.*

THE BRITISH BIOGRAPHICAL READER:

Brief Biographies of prominent British Heroes, Statesmen, Dramatists, Poets, Scientific Men, &c. Illustrated by numerous Portraits. Foolscap 8vo, cloth extra, 2s. 6d.

"A number of excellent portraits add considerably to the attractiveness of the work, which may safely be pronounced one of the most interesting of the Series."—*Aberdeen Journal.*

LONDON, PAST AND PRESENT.

Being Notices Historical and Descriptive of Ancient and Modern London. With Illustrations. F'cap 8vo, cloth extra, 2s. 6d.

"A compilation from which a variety of interesting information may be gathered with regard to the past history and present condition of the metropolis."—*Athenæum.*

THE WINGS OF COURAGE,

AND THE CLOUD-SPINNER. Translated from the French of GEORGE SAND, by MRS. CORKRAN. With 2 coloured Illustrations. Small 8vo, cloth extra, 2s.

These stories are among the most attractive of the many tales which the great French novelist wrote for her grandchildren. Hitherto the juvenile stories told by George Sand have been little known in this country, but they are so full of fancy, of vivid description, and of a keen appreciation of the best way to arouse the interest of juvenile readers that it is time they were introduced here. The romantic manner in which they are told lends to them the kind of enchantment which thoughtful children deeply appreciate.

FOUR LITTLE MISCHIEFS.

By ROSA MULHOLLAND, author of "Five Little Farmers," &c. With 3 full-page Pictures in colours. Cr. 8vo, cloth extra, 2s.

This story of child-life is one of the most amusing of the author's excellent little books. Its fun is innocent, its incident both captivating and instructive.

"Will be read with absorbing interest by the youngsters."—*Land and Water.*

OUR DOLLY:

Her Words and Ways. By Mrs. R. H. READ. With many Woodcuts, and a Frontispiece in colours. Cr. 8vo, cloth extra, 2s.

A story for children, showing the growth and development of character in a little girl, and describing the surroundings of the family and a series of entertaining small adventures suitable for very juvenile readers.

"Prettily told and prettily illustrated."—*Guardian.*

FAIRY FANCY:

What she Heard and what she Saw. By Mrs. R. H. READ. With many Woodcut Illustrations in the text, and a Frontispiece printed in colours. Crown 8vo, cloth elegant, price 2s.

The tale is designed to show the influence of character even among little children, and the narrative is such as to awaken and sustain the interest of the younger readers.

"The authoress has very great insight into child nature, and a sound healthy tone pervades the book."—*Glasgow Herald.*

"All is pleasant, nice reading, with a little knowledge of natural history and other dry matters gently introduced and divested of dryness."—*Practical Teacher.*

ADVENTURES OF MRS. WISHING-TO-BE.

By ALICE CORKRAN, author of "Latheby Towers," &c. With 3
full-page Pictures in colours. Crown 8vo, cloth extra, 2s.

The strange adventures of a very young lady, showing how she met with
the wonderful people of nursery legend and the manner of her introduction
to them. A tale for the Little Ones.

"Simply a charming book for little girls. We have a good deal of confidence in
recommending the book, which is, moreover, well illustrated."—*Saturday Review.*

NAUGHTY MISS BUNNY:

Her Tricks and Troubles. A Story for Little Children. With
3 Illustrations in colours. By CLARA MULHOLLAND. Crown
8vo, cloth extra, price 2s.

This is a book which will amuse quite little folks, as a story of the way-
ward tricks of a spoiled child, and the scrapes into which they lead her.
The story consists of small incidents such as please small listeners, who will
be interested not only in Miss Bunny's naughtiness, but in her reformation.

"This naughty child is positively delightful. Papas should not omit 'Naughty
Miss Bunny' from their list of juvenile presents."—*Land and Water.*

NEW LIGHT THROUGH OLD WINDOWS.

A Series of Stories illustrating Fables of Æsop. By GREGSON
Gow. With 3 full-page Pictures in colours. Crown 8vo, cloth
extra, 2s.

A series of stories designed to bring before the young mind, in a new
and entertaining form, some of the shreds of wit and wisdom which have
come down to us from ancient times in the guise of fables. Although
amusement has been a chief end aimed at, most of the tales will be found
to suggest some important truth, or teach some sound lesson in practical
morality.

"Racy, pointed, and fitted to delight young folks."—*Freeman.*
"Entertaining for young and old alike."—*Life.*

MADGE'S MISTAKE.

A Recollection of Girlhood. By ANNIE E. ARMSTRONG. With
2 coloured Illustrations. Small 8vo, cloth extra, 1s. 6d.

This is a lively, interesting little story, the characters are well marked,
and the plot, although simple, is so well worked out as to lead the reader,
young or old, on to the last word.

TROUBLES AND TRIUMPHS OF LITTLE TIM.

A City Story. By GREGSON Gow, author of "Tales for the
Twilight." With two Illustrations in colour. Foolscap 8vo,
192 pp., cloth extra, 1s. 6d.

"Strong in character and full of incident, and the narrative all through is interesting and touching."—*Edinburgh Daily Review.*

"An unmistakable undercurrent of sympathy with the struggles of the poor, and
an ability to describe their feelings under various circumstances, eminently characteristic of Dickens, are marked features in Mr. Gow's story."—*North British Mail.*

THE HAPPY LAD.

A Story of Peasant Life in Norway. From the Norwegian of
Björnstjerne Björnson. With Frontispiece in colour. Foolscap 8vo, 192 pp., cloth extra, 1s. 6d.

"The lad is happy from being a plucky boy, a good son, and a successful lover."—
Glasgow Herald.

INTO THE HAVEN.

By ANNIE S. SWAN, author of "Shadow Lives," "Thankful Rest,"
&c. With two Illustrations printed in colour. Foolscap 8vo,
192 pp., cloth extra, 1s. 6d.

"No story more attractive . . . by reason of its breezy freshness and unforced
pathos, as well as for the wholesome practical lessons it conveys."—*Christian Leader.*

BOX OF STORIES.

Packed for Young Folk by HORACE HAPPYMAN. A Series of
interesting Tales for the Young. With 2 Illustrations printed
in colours. Foolscap 8vo, 192 pp., cloth extra, 1s. 6d.

JEANNE D'ARC, THE PATRIOT MARTYR:

And other Narratives of Female Heroism in Peace and War.
Illustrated by 2 Pictures printed in colours. Foolscap 8vo,
cloth extra, 1s. 6d.

THE NEW BOY AT MERRITON.

By JULIA GODDARD. With Frontispiece in colour. F'cap 8vo,
128 pp., cloth extra, price 1s.

"A story of English school life. It is an attempt to teach a somewhat higher code
of honour than that which prevails among the general run of schoolboys, and the
lesson makes a very good story."—*School Board Chronicle.*

THE BLIND BOY OF DRESDEN.

With Frontispiece in colour. F'cap 8vo, 128 pp., cloth extra,
price 1s.

"This is a family story of great pathos. It does not obtrusively dictate its lesson,
but it quietly introduces, and leaves it within the heart."—*Aberdeen Journal.*

JON OF ICELAND:

A True Story. With Frontispiece in colour. F'cap 8vo, 128 pp.,
cloth extra, price 1s.

"'Jon of Iceland' is a sturdy, well educated young Icelander, who becomes a successful teacher. It gives children a clear idea of the chief physical features of the
island, and of the simple and manly character of its inhabitants."—*School Guardian.*

STORIES FROM SHAKESPEARE.

By MACFARLAND and ABBY SAGE. With Frontispiece in colour.
F'cap 8vo, 128 pp., cloth extra, price 1s.

"The stories are told in such a way that young people having read them will desire
to study the works of Shakespeare in their original form."—*The Schoolmistress.*

EVERY MAN IN HIS PLACE:

The Story of a City Boy and a Forest Boy. With Frontispiece
in colour. F'cap 8vo, 128 pp., cloth extra, price 1s.

"This is the history of the son of a wealthy Hamburg merchant, who wished to
follow in the steps of Robinson Crusoe. He visited Heligoland and the Hartz Mountains, and was put to the test, and became convinced in the end that it is better to
live the life of a wealthy merchant in a great city than to endure hardship by choice."
—*School Board Chronicle.*

FIRESIDE FAIRIES AND FLOWER FANCIES:

STORIES FOR GIRLS. With Frontispiece in colour. F'cap 8vo, 128 pp., cloth extra, price 1*s.*

"Nine stories are included, all for girls, encouraging them to try and do their duty. Young servants would find this book very interesting."—*The Schoolmistress.*

TO THE SEA IN SHIPS:

STORIES OF SUFFERING AND SAVING AT SEA. With Frontispiece in colour. F'cap 8vo, 128 pp., cloth extra, price 1*s.*

"*To the Sea in Ships* records several noted disasters at sea, such as the foundering of the *London* and the wreck of the *Atlantic.* It also contains narratives of successful rescues. This is a capital book for boys."—*School Guardian.*

JACK'S VICTORY:

AND OTHER STORIES ABOUT DOGS. With Frontispiece in colour. F'cap 8vo, 128 pp., cloth extra, price 1*s.*

"Every boy, and some girls, take great delight in reading about dogs. Well, Jack was a dog; a famous and wonderful one, too. He became leader of a team in Greenland, and some rare exploits he took part in. He would not sleep in a house; he would not hide from an enemy; he would not harm the defenceless. Besides 'Jack's Victory' there are ten other stories about dogs in this volume. These narratives are not old ones, but are fresh and pleasing."—*The Schoolmistress.*

THE STORY OF A KING,

TOLD BY ONE OF HIS SOLDIERS. With Frontispiece in colour. F'cap 8vo, 128 pp., cloth extra, price 1*s.*

"This book recounts the boyhood and reign of Charles XII. of Sweden. The wars in which he was engaged and the extraordinary victories he won are well described, and equally so are the misfortunes which latterly came on him and his kingdom through his uncontrollable wilfulness."—*Aberdeen Journal.*

LITTLE DANIEL:

A Story of a Flood on the Rhine. With Frontispiece in colour.
F'cap 8vo, 128 pp., cloth extra, price 1s.

"A simple and touching story of a flood on the Rhine, told as well as George
Eliot so graphically wrote of *The Mill on the Floss.*"—*Governess.*

PRINCE ALEXIS:

A Tale of Old Russia. With Frontispiece in colour. F'cap 8vo,
128 pp., cloth extra, price 1s.

This is a legend wrought into a story, rendering a fiction of Life in
Russia, something more than a hundred years ago; a state of things which,
as the author says, "is now impossible, and will soon become incredible."
It is like a romance of Old Bagdad, in which the colouring and the characters and manners are Russian instead of Arabian.

SASHA THE SERF,

And other Stories of Russian Life. With Frontispiece in colour.
F'cap 8vo, 128 pp., cloth extra, price 1s.

The stories in the volume comprise:—The Life of Sasha, a poor boy who,
by his love of knowledge and his industry, saved the life of his lord, and
finally rose to wealth and gained his freedom,—Incidents of remarkable
personal bravery in the Russian army,—An interesting story of humble life
in Russia,—A story of Russian mining life,—A bear-hunt in Russia, &c. &c.

TRUE STORIES OF FOREIGN HISTORY.

A Series of Interesting Tales. With Frontispiece printed in
colours. F'cap 8vo, 128 pp., cloth extra, price 1s.

The book contains stories—Of some of the early printers,—How Quentin
Matsys the Antwerp smith became a great painter,—The rise and fall
of Jean Ango the fisherman of Dieppe,—The early trials of Fritz Körner
the tailor's son, who could not learn his father's trade but who became
commander-in-chief of the Brunswick forces,—Of Polish patriotism,—The
heroism of Casabianca the little French midshipman, &c. &c.

THE LITTLE BROWN BIRD:

A Story of Industry. With Frontispiece in colours. Medium
8vo, cloth elegant, price 6*d*.

This book contains two tales, the first intended to inculcate habits of
industry, and the other to show that mediocrity with perseverance achieves
a more honourable career than "talent" wasted or misapplied.

THE MAID OF DOMREMY:

And other Tales. With Frontispiece in colours. Medium 8vo,
cloth elegant, price 6*d*.

"The Maid of Domremy" is in fact Joan of Arc, whose story is well rendered into something less than twenty pages. Other sections of the little
volume treat of the "Feast of Cherries;" "Something about Royal Children;" "The Black Douglas;" "What a Boy Did," and "Johanna Sebus."
These are all narratives of fact.

LITTLE ERIC:

A Story of Honesty. With Frontispiece in colours. Medium 8vo,
cloth elegant, price 6*d*.

This is a pure juvenile fiction, illustrative of truthfulness and honesty.
It is full of interest from beginning to end, and well suited as a reward
book for Sunday Schools.

UNCLE BEN THE WHALER:

And other Stories. With Frontispiece in colours. Medium 8vo,
cloth elegant, price 6*d*.

"Uncle Ben the Whaler" is an "old salt" who tells a group of children
a very interesting tale of his career as a seaman in the Arctic waters. The
other stories in the volume are:—Three Handfuls of Grain,—The Golden
Rule,—The Broken Jar.

THE PALACE OF LUXURY:

And other Stories. With Frontispiece in colours. Medium 8vo, cloth elegant, price 6*d*.

A youth named Seekpeace is shown under the guidance of the fairy Pureheart all the deceptions in the Palace of Luxury,—Madam Sunshine's parable about the Swan of Fortune,—The Colorado beetle's talk with the weathercock,—and other short amusing stories.

THE CHARCOAL BURNER:

Or Kindness Repaid. With Frontispiece in colours. Medium 8vo, cloth elegant, price 6*d*.

This is a most interesting story of a poor charcoal-burner in a German forest, who discovers and relieves a wounded officer, and is himself afterwards strangely delivered from death by the same officer. The tale inculcates the duty of always showing kindness and of forgiving an injury.

WILLIE BLACK:

A Story of Doing Right. With Frontispiece in colours. Medium 8vo, cloth elegant, price 6*d*.

It is a tale of a little Shoe-black to whom a gentleman gave half-a-crown by mistake for a penny, and it shows all the good that came to this little boy through seeking to restore the silver coin to its owner. Proving how it is always best to do right.

THE HORSE AND HIS WAYS:

Stories of Man and his Best Friend. With Frontispiece in colours. Medium 8vo, cloth elegant, price 6*d*.

A series of interesting anecdotes about the courage of the horse; its friendship, its docility, its sagacity, and its power of memory.

THE SHOEMAKER'S PRESENT:

A Legendary Story. With Frontispiece in colours. Medium 8vo,
cloth elegant, price 6*d*.

A legendary story of "How a boy became obedient." The tale is told
in a semi-magical tone, and is very interesting.

LIGHTS TO WALK BY:

Stories for the Young. With Frontispiece in colours. Medium
8vo, cloth elegant, price 6*d*.

The book contains: Willy Montague's Lesson—The Visit of the Prince—
The Conscript of Lyons—My Friend Jacques—Honesty and Usefulness—
God's Promise. They are all lively little narratives, each with a wholesome
moral. They are well written and very attractive.

THE LITTLE MERCHANT:

And other Stories. With Frontispiece in colours. Medium 8vo,
cloth elegant, price 6*d*.

This book contains a series of little stories of English life and of the
experience of young people in this land. They are all designed to enforce
some important moral lesson, such as honesty, industry, kindness, &c. &c.

NICHOLINA:

A Story about an Iceberg. With Frontispiece in colours. Medium
8vo, cloth elegant, price 6*d*.

This is a tale of the Arctic regions, full of peculiar interest and vividly
suggestive of the feeling which is conveyed to the mind of the traveller
who wanders over these latitudes. The other stories in the volume are:—
Frozen in; a Story of the Arctic Circle,—Idana and Her Apples; a Story
of Iceland.

A NEW SERIES

OF

FOURPENNY REWARD BOOKS.

Each 64 Pages, 18mo, Illustrated, in Picture Boards.

BRAVE AND TRUE. By GREGSON GOW.

POOR TOM OLLIVER. By JULIA GODDARD.

THE CHILDREN AND THE WATER-LILY. By JULIA GODDARD.

JOHNNIE TUPPER'S TEMPTATION. By GREGSON GOW.

FRITZ'S EXPERIMENT. By LETITIA M'CLINTOCK.

CLIMBING THE HILL. By ANNIE S. SWAN.

A YEAR AT COVERLEY. By ANNIE S. SWAN.

LUCY'S CHRISTMAS-BOX: OR, HOW GEORGIE FOUND HIS COUSIN.

** These little books have been specially written with the aim of inculcating some sound moral, such as obedience to parents, love for brothers and sisters, kindness to animals, perseverance and diligence leading to success, &c. &c.

VERE FOSTER'S
WATER-COLOR DRAWING-BOOKS.

SIMPLE LESSONS IN WATER-COLOR.

A series of Eight Fac-similes of Original Water-Color Drawings, and Thirty Vignettes, after various artists. With full instructions by an experienced Master. In Four Parts small 4to, price 6*d*. each, or one volume, cloth elegant, 3*s.*

EASY STUDIES IN WATER-COLOR PAINTING.

By R. P. LEITCH and J. CALLOW. A series of Nine Pictures executed in Neutral Tints. With full instructions for drawing each subject, and for Sketching from Nature. In Three Parts 4to, 1*s*. 6*d*. each, or one volume, cloth elegant, 6*s.*

SKETCHES IN WATER-COLORS.

By T. M. RICHARDSON, R. P. LEITCH, J. A. HOUSTON, T. L. ROW-BOTHAM, E. DUNCAN, and J. NEEDHAM. A series of Nine Pictures executed in colors. With full instructions for drawing each subject, by an experienced Teacher. In Three Parts 4to, 1*s*. 6*d*. each, or one volume, cloth elegant, 6*s.*

"The paper, printing, and general get-up of the series leave nothing to be desired."—*Educational Times.*

"To those who wish to become proficient in the art of water-color painting no better instructor could be recommended than these series."—*Newcastle Chronicle.*

"Deserve the highest commendation; they are extremely serviceable for their purpose, and are got up with remarkable care."—*St. James's Gazette.*

"The names of the artists are quite sufficient to stamp these books with the highest qualities. The pictures are judicious in selection and artistic in execution, while the instructions are so full and clear as to almost supersede the need of a teacher."—*Liverpool Courier.*

"A better selection of sketches calculated to guide the pupil in his progress with the brush could scarcely have been made."—*Bristol Mercury.*

BLOCKS FORMED OF STOUT PAPER PREPARED FOR
SKETCHING FROM NATURE.

No. 1 (6½" × 4½"), Threepence.   No. 2 (9" × 6½"), Sixpence.

Approved by the Science and Art Department, South Kensington.

VERE FOSTER'S DRAWING COPY-BOOKS.

With Instructions and Paper to draw on. SUPERIOR EDITION, in Numbers,
at 3*d.* POPULAR EDITION (a selection) at 1*d.* COMPLETE EDITION, in Twelve
Parts, at 1*s.* (Each part complete in itself.)

Part I.—ELEMENTARY.

A 1 Initiatory Lessons.
A 2 Letters and Numerals.
B 1 Familiar Objects (Straight Lines).
B 2 Domestic Objects (Simple).

Part II.—OBJECTS.

C 1 Domestic Objects (Flat).
C 2 Domestic Objects (Perspective).
D 1 Leaves (Flat).
D 2 Leaves (Natural).

Part III.—PLANTS.

E 1 Plants (Simple Forms).
E 2 Plants (More Complex Forms).
G 1 Flowers (Simple Forms).
G 2 Flowers (More Complex Forms).

Part IV.—ORNAMENT.

I 1 Elementary Forms.
I 2 Simple Forms (Fretwork, Ironwork, &c.).
I 3 Advanced (Carving, Sculpture, &c.).
I 4 Ornament (Classic, Renaissance, &c.).

Part V.—TREES.

J 1 Oak, Fir, &c., with "touch" for each tree.
J 2 Beech, Elm, &c., do. do.
J 3 Oak, Chestnut, Birch, &c., do. do.
J 4 Larch, Poplar, Lime, Willow, &c., do.

Part VI.—LANDSCAPE.

K 1 Rustic Landscape in Outline.
K 2 Shaded Objects and Landscape.
K 3 Shaded Landscape and Rustic Scenes.
K 4 Advanced Landscape and Rural Scenes.

Part VII.—MARINE.

M 1 Boats, Foregrounds, and Nautical Bits.
M 2 Fishing Craft, Coasters, and Traders.
M 3 Yachts and Vessels of every Rig and Sail.
M 4 Coast Scenes, Waves, &c.

Parts VIII. and IX.—ANIMALS.

O 1 Birds and Quadrupeds.
O 2 Poultry, various breeds.
O 3 British Small Birds.
O 4 British Wild Animals.
O 5 Horses (Arab, Hunter, Dray, &c.).
O 6 Horses (Racer, Trotter, Pony, Mule, &c.).
O 7 Dogs (Seventeen Species).
O 8 Cattle, Sheep, Pigs, Goats, &c.
O 9 Cattle, Sheep, Lambs, Ass and Foal, &c.
O 10 Foreign Wild Animals and Birds.

Part X.—HUMAN FIGURE.

Q 1 Features (from the Antique and from the Life).
Q 2 Heads, Hands, &c. (from Cast and Life).
Q 3 Rustic Figures, by Duncan.
Q 4 Figure, from the Antique (Outline).

Part XI.—PRACTICAL GEOMETRY.

R 1 Definitions and Simple Problems.
R 2 Practical Geometry (Circle, Polygon, Ellipse).
R 3 Applied Geometry *for Practical Mechanics, &c.*

Part XII.—MECHANICAL DRAWING.

T 1 Initiatory and Simple Subjects.
T 2 Details of Tools and Working Parts, &c.
T 3 Models for Working Drawings, &c.
T 4 Details of Machines and Engines.
Z BLANK EXERCISE BOOK.

Popular Edition, a selection of the above numbers printed on thin paper, price
1*d.* each number. The following are in print:—A, B, C, D, E2, E3, G, I1, I2, I3,
I4, J2, K1, M1, M4, O7, O8, O9, O10, Q, R1, R2, R3, R4, T1, T5, T6, T7, T8, Z.

"If any parent who reads these lines has a boy or girl who wishes to learn how
to be an artist, let us boldly recommend Vere Foster's Drawing Book. It is not
only the cheapest but by far the best that we have seen."—*Graphic.*
"It would be difficult to over-rate the value of this work—a work that is not
to be estimated by its cost: one is great, the other very small."—*Art Journal.*

NATIONAL COMPETITION IN WRITING AND DRAWING.

MR. VERE FOSTER has awarded prizes for Writing and Drawing for many years.
4550 Prizes, in sums of from 5*s.* to £5, have been already distributed, amounting
to about £2000. List of prize-takers for last year and scheme for the Fourteenth
Annual Competition, 1884, will be sent post free on application to MR. VERE
FOSTER, Belfast, or to the Publishers.

Sanctioned by the Committee of Council on Education.

POYNTER'S
SOUTH KENSINGTON DRAWING-BOOK.

This new series of Drawing-Books has been issued under the direct superintendence of E. J. POYNTER, R.A., who has selected the examples for the most part from objects in the South Kensington Museum. The original Drawings have been made under Mr. Poynter's supervision by Pupils of the National Art Training School.

Freehand Drawing.

Each Book has Fine Cartridge Paper to draw on.

Freehand, Elementary. Simple Forms, Leaves, and Flowers. Four Books, 6d. each.

Freehand, First Grade. Simple Objects, Ornament (Flat and Perspective). Six Books, 6d. each.

Freehand, Second Grade. Ornament (Greek, Renaissance, &c.). Four Books, 1s. each.

THE SAME SUBJECTS ON CARDS.

Elementary Freehand Cards, Four Packets, price 9d. each.
First Grade Freehand Cards, Six „ „ 1s. 0d. „ .
Second Grade Freehand Cards, Four „ „ 1s. 6d. „

"The choice of subjects is admirable; there is not an ugly drawing in the book, and the infinite variety of curves that may be found in glass-work, porcelain, shells, scroll-work, musical instruments, &c., is illustrated with great skill in Mr. Poynter's models."—*Pall Mall Gazette.*

"Mr. Poynter's is probably the best series of the kind yet published."—*The Academy.*

Elementary Human Figure.

Each Book has Fine Cartridge Paper to draw on.

Book I.—MICHAEL ANGELO'S "DAVID"—Features (Eye, Nose, etc.). Price Sixpence.
Books II. and III.—HANDS AND FEET. *In preparation.*

The subjects of these books are taken from actual examples in the South Kensington Museum. They are executed in *fac-simile* of charcoal drawings.

Elementary Perspective Drawing.

By S. J. CARTLIDGE, Lecturer in the National Art Training School, South Kensington. Four Books, 1s. each.

Book I. } For II. Grade Examination of the Department. *Just ready.*
Book II. }

Book III.—ACCIDENTAL VANISHING POINTS. } *In active preparation.*
Book IV.—HIGHER PERSPECTIVE. }

BOOKS FOR YOUNG READERS

SUITABLE FOR PRIZES, REWARDS, GIFTS, &c.

Classified according to Price.

ALL ELEGANTLY BOUND IN EXTRA CLOTH.

Book at 7s. 6d.

The Universe; or, The Infinitely Great and Infinitely Little. By F. A. POUCHET, M.D

Books at 6s.

With Clive in India. By G. A. HENTY.

The Golden Magnet. By G. MANVILLE FENN.

In the King's Name. By G. MANVILLE FENN.

Under Drake's Flag. By G. A. HENTY.

Easy Studies in Water-Color, with Coloured Plates.

Sketches in Water-Color, with Plates.

Books at 5s.

By Sheer Pluck. By G. A. HENTY.

The Wigwam and the War-Path. By ASCOTT R. HOPE.

Facing Death. By G. A. HENTY.

Stories of Old Renown. By ASCOTT R. HOPE. Illustrated by GORDON BROWNE.

Nat the Naturalist. By G. MANVILLE FENN.

Books at 3s. 6d.

Cheep and Chatter. By ALICE BANKS.

Picked up at Sea. By J. C. HUTCHESON.

Dr. Jolliffe's Boys. By LEWIS HOUGH.

Brother and Sister. By Mrs. LYSAGHT.

Dora. By Mrs. R. H. READ.

Garnered Sheaves. By Mrs. E. R. PITMAN.

Life's Daily Ministry. By Mrs. PITMAN.

Florence Godfrey's Faith. By Mrs. PITMAN.

My Governess Life. By Mrs. PITMAN.

Unravelled Skeins. By GREGSON GOW.

Myths and Legends of Ancient Greece and Rome.

Book at 3s.

Simple Lessons in Water-Color, with Plates.

Books at 2s. 6d.

Jack o' Lanthorn. By HENRY FRITH.

A Waif of the Sea. By KATE WOOD.

Hetty Gray. By ROSA MULHOLLAND.

The Ball of Fortune. By CHAS. PEARCE.

The Family Failing. By DARLEY DALE.

Episodes of the Sea in Former Days.

Episodes of Foreign Life and Manners.

Episodes of Captivity and Exile.

Episodes of Personal Adventure.

Episodes of History.

Episodes of Discovery in all Ages.

The Newspaper Reader.

The British Biographical Reader.

London Past and Present.

Books at 2s.

The Wings of Courage. By GEORGE SAND.

Four Little Mischiefs. By ROSA MULHOLLAND.

Our Dolly. By Mrs. R. H. READ.

Fairy Fancy. By Mrs. R. H. READ.

Mrs. Wishing-to-be. By ALICE CORKRAN.

New Light through Old Windows. By GREGSON GOW.

Naughty Miss Bunny. By CLARA MULHOLLAND.

Books at 1s. 6d.

Madge's Mistake. By ANNIE E. ARMSTRONG.

Troubles and Triumphs of Little Tim. By GREGSON GOW.

The Happy Lad. By BJÖRNSON.

Into the Haven. By ANNIE S. SWAN.

Box of Stories. Packed by HORACE HAPPYMAN.

The Patriot Martyr: and other Narratives of Female Heroism.

Books at 1s.

The New Boy at Merriton.

The Blind Boy of Dresden and his Sister.

Jon of Iceland: A True Story.

Stories from Shakespeare.

Every Man in His Place.

Fireside Fairies and Flower Fancies.

To the Sea in Ships.

Little Daniel: a Story of a Flood on the Rhine.

Jack's Victory: and other Stories about Dogs.

The Story of a King: told by one of his Soldiers.

Prince Alexis, or "Beauty and the Beast."

Sasha the Serf: Stories of Russian Life.

True Stories of Foreign History.

Books at 6d.

The Little Brown Bird: a Story of Industry.

The Maid of Domremy: and other Tales.

Little Eric: a Story of Honesty.

Uncle Ben the Whaler: and other Stories.

The Palace of Luxury: and other Stories.

The Charcoal-Burner: or, Kindness Repaid.

Willy Black: a Story of Doing Right.

The Horse and his Ways.

The Shoemaker's Present: a Legendary Story.

Lights to Walk by: Stories for the Young.

The Little Merchant: and other Stories.

Nicholina: a Story about an Iceberg.

Books at 4d.

Brave and True. By GREGSON GOW.

Poor Tom Olliver. By JULIA GODDARD.

The Children and the Water-Lily. By JULIA GODDARD.

Johnnie Tupper's Temptation. By GREGSON GOW.

Fritz's Experiment. By LETITIA M'CLINTOCK.

Climbing the Hill. By ANNIE S. SWAN.

A Year at Coverley. By ANNIE S. SWAN.

Lucy's Christmas-Box; or, How Georgie found his Cousin.

LONDON: BLACKIE & SON, 49 OLD BAILEY, E.C.;
GLASGOW, EDINBURGH, AND DUBLIN.

www.ingramcontent.com/pod-product-compliance
Lightning Source LLC
Chambersburg PA
CBHW030320270326
41926CB00010B/1435